Praise for *Unleash the Girls*

"The sports bra was and is more than a piece of sporting equipment, it has become a symbol and a vehicle for women and girls to propel themselves forward without inhibition towards the future that they are creating. Prior to its inception, the concept of women running, jumping, lifting, competing, basically moving dynamically, caused reticence. NOW, WE RUN AND MOVE in every athletic space and then some. To say I don't think about my sports bra anymore is to say that I am FREE to accomplish and go after anything I want. I am EMPOWERED TO EMBRACE OPPORTUNITY!"

—*Brandi Chastain, American retired soccer player, two-time FIFA Women's World Cup champion, two-time Olympic gold-medalist, coach, and sports broadcaster*

"With cogent reflections on American cultural history and the shifts that laid the groundwork for women's liberation, Lindahl weaves a narrative that is both intimate and topical....[A]n inspiring narrative about changing the world through fearless innovation."

—*Publisher's Weekly, BookLife Prize*

"The introduction of the sports bra did more than improve athletic performance. It represented a revolution in ready-to-wear clothing, and for many women athletes—past, present, and future—it actually made sports possible."

—*Smithsonian Museum of American History Archivist Cathy Keen*

UNLEASH THE GIRLS

The Untold Story of the Invention of the Sports
Bra and How It Changed the World (and Me)

LISA Z. LINDAHL

Disclaimer:

This work depicts actual events in the life of the author as truthfully as recollection permits and/or can be verified by research. Occasionally, dialogue consistent with the character or nature of the person speaking has been supplemented. All persons within are actual individuals; there are no composite characters. The names of some individuals have been changed or only partially included to respect their privacy.

Hardback ISBN: 978-1-647040-06-2
Paperback ISBN: 978-1-950282-43-2
eBook ISBN: 978-1-950282-44-9

Covering the bases: "Jogbra" is now a trademark of HBI Branded Apparel Enterprises, LLC, Winston Salem, NC

Distributed by Bublish, Inc.
Cover Design by Berge Design

TABLE OF CONTENTS

PREFACE

Sometimes, a single moment captures and reveals the essence of your life's purpose. For me, it happened one day near the end of winter in Vermont. It was not quite springtime—"mud season," as it's called—a difficult time of year for souls yearning for sunshine's warmth and the first signs of green. I was standing at the window of my studio office overlooking Lake Champlain—always a changeable, capricious view. This day, I noticed a wind was tickling the top of the lake's slate-colored surface. But my attention was turned inward. I was wrestling with my identity and how the title "successful businesswoman" fit into the whole of my life. I chafed under the typical introduction of "Meet Lisa, the Jogbra Lady!" Wasn't I more than just this one achievement? Had my entrepreneurial journey made a difference in the world? Did any of it really matter?

Nature, as she always did, called me back. Outside my window, the gray sky was beginning to lift, and just enough midday light was filtering through to create a bright and otherworldly sparkle on the lake's now choppy water. The light silhouetted the dark tree branches lining the lake's edge, highlighting the baby yellow leaf buds clinging there. A blue jay's call pierced my silence, and suddenly I was immersed—if only for a moment—in a deep sense of timeless and complete beauty.

There was my answer.

In that moment, I realized that what really mattered was *beauty*. Not physical beauty. Not glamour, which is so often confused with beauty in today's culture. No, what I had experienced was much bigger. It was *True Beauty*, transcendent and everlasting.

Since that moment, I've made it my life's work to learn the way of True Beauty and teach others how to find and experience it and use it to create greater harmony in our world.

My journey to that life-changing moment on Lake Champlain was long and circuitous. It began in a very different time and place—a time when my relationship with myself was muddled and my understanding of beauty was still nascent. I was a young, artistic woman trying to find herself. It was the early 1970s, and we were all trying to find ourselves. The "women's liberation movement," as it was then called, had swept across the United States. The changes were so profound that *Time* magazine awarded its 1975 "Man of the Year" cover to "American Women." Only two years earlier, tennis star Billy Jean King had captivated the nation's attention when she beat Bobby Riggs in the "Battle of the Sexes" on the tennis court. Women were coming into their own, working hard to carve out new roles for themselves at home and in sports, culture, politics, and business.

The nation in general was also beginning to move. We were getting up off the couch, where we'd been watching TV shows like *All in the Family*, *Maude*, *M*A*S*H*, and *Bewitched*, and joining the "fitness revolution." People started jogging—en masse. It's estimated that twenty-five million Americans took up running in the 1970s and 1980s, including President Jimmy Carter.

It's at this unique intersection between feminism and athleticism that my entrepreneurial story began. With the passage of Title IX in 1972, which prohibited discrimination on the basis of sex in any federally funded education program, doors were finally opening for young women not only in the classroom but also on the field. But Title IX could not erase the discomfort and self-consciousness that were insidious ingredients in keeping girls and women off those fields.

Along with the other young women of my "baby boomer" generation, I was trying to find my way. In my midtwenties I had headed back to the college classroom and, as part of my self-reinvention, had taken up jogging. My new love of running, though, came with a problem: my breasts bounced—a lot. It was a constant distraction and discomfort and the only thing not great about my runs. I needed a solution.

When I invented the sports bra in 1977, it completed what Title IX had started. It leveled the playing field for female athletes and athletic women. It turned out to be the one-two punch that knocked out old attitudes and restrictions. You might even say it "unleashed the girls."

The Jogbra files, prototype, and history are now preserved at the Smithsonian Museum of American History, where archivist Cathy Keen said in 2015, "The introduction of the sports bra did more than improve athletes' performances. It represented a revolution in ready-to-wear clothing, and for many women athletes—past, present, and future—it actually made sports possible."

The original Jogbra company's slogan was "by women, for women." I believe that women's stories must be told and—when possible—by the women who lived the tale. The story of the invention of the first sports bra is very much a story of women. It is also a big part of my life story. This is the improbable story of how I created the first sports bra and how it changed the world—as well as the course of my life.

1.
INSPIRED

"A small group of thoughtful people could change the world.
Indeed, it's the only thing that ever has."
~ Margaret Mead

L et's face it, in 1977, I was an unlikely candidate to become a business success story, let alone change the world for women in sports, especially seeing as I'd never been particularly athletic. My formal business education consisted of a postcollegiate, one-year program at the Katharine Gibbs Secretarial School. I was an aspiring artist, working in stained glass and selling my work at craft fairs. At the same time, I was working part-time at Threshold, a rural, residential treatment facility for adolescent drug abusers where my husband, Al, worked as a counselor. I administered tests and did secretarial stuff. I had little interest in a nine-to-five sort of traditional career. At twenty-eight, I was working on finishing my undergraduate degree at the University of Vermont (UVM) in Burlington, my marriage of seven years to Al was shaky, and I couldn't drive a car due to having epilepsy. It was quite an odd resume.

At the time, my lack of mobility felt like a greater disability to me than having the occasional epileptic seizure. Without a driver's license in our car-centric world, I was very dependent on others. I could only maintain the job at Threshold because I got a ride out to its very rural location with Al. This aspect of my epilepsy-induced dependence was probably one reason I had married so early and was certainly a factor in my decision in 1977 to take yet another job, this time as a low-level filing clerk at the UVM admissions office. It was hard on my ego and horribly boring, but, unlike the job at the drug treatment facility, it was within walking distance of my house and afforded me a free academic course each semester. As an "older woman" in her late twenties (ha!), I was intimidated by the prospect of going back to college. This job afforded me a way to try it out, then literally to make it more affordable.

Sitting most of the day for my filing job, I began to put on weight. My once "drop-dead gorgeous" figure, taken for granted ever since its appearance around age fifteen, had become blowzy and indistinct. A friend told me what I somehow knew but had resisted: dieting alone wouldn't shed the pounds. I would need to exercise. My friend outlined his running regime, telling me that all I had to do was run a mile and a quarter three times a week and I would achieve and maintain "physical fitness." To me, translated, that meant "skinny." And Lord knows, as a 1960s teenage girl, skinny was a beauty hallmark. Remember Twiggy? Count me in.

The UVM job also gave me access to the university's athletic facilities. Every day during my tightly controlled, exactly sixty-minute lunch hour, I walked up to the field house to run. The indoor track there was only one-tenth of a mile, but it might as well have been a thousand miles long. That first day, I could barely make it around even once. But my competitive spirit was awakened—and I suppose vanity drove me forward as well. I was determined to shed that creeping weight. Each day, I pushed myself to go just a little farther. Just . . . a . . . little . . . farther. Until the day, months later, when I finally completed the tenth consecutive lap for the first time. I was elated. I had run an entire mile! You would have thought I'd won an Olympic gold medal. I felt terrific. I had challenged myself and won!

A little background here. My mother, raised by her Victorian-era grandmother, was a firm believer that her daughters would be raised to be *ladies*. Always full of platitudes, with such wisdom she would intone, "Horses sweat, men perspire, ladies glow." Athletics, let alone organized sports, were not part of her repertoire. Me? Give me a bathing suit and point me toward ocean surf. No boards, please. Growing up, spending my summers on the New Jersey shore—that was my idea of being "active." But in my midtwenties, living in landlocked Vermont, there was no ocean nearby. When I found jogging, it became my land-based equivalent of active joy.

My running never grew into a desire to compete. Rather, running reconnected me to the natural world and became, frankly, one of my first spiritual practices. It is totally ironic that this practice spawned my financial success and exposure to the grit of the business world. And in so doing, like all good spiritual practices, it afforded me the opportunity to confront some difficult personal issues. Oh, joy!

The deeper irony is that for me to start running at all was completely out of character, Mom's "encouragement" notwithstanding. While I remember enjoying recess and dodgeball in elementary school, by middle school at the girls' academy I attended, I was self-conscious and uncomfortable in gym classes. A 2019 study shows that many girls still feel awkward in gym class, but back in the early '60s, all I knew was that my best friend Polly and I definitely were. We hated those moments in the locker room! There were those "jock" girls who relished gym and understood the rules of field hockey and were eager to get out on the tennis courts. They intimidated me. It seemed to me that I was somehow less for not "getting" the whole sporty thing and for being so self-conscious. When possible, I opted for Beginning Bowling as my gym class choice. I didn't even like to glow, let alone perspire. When I look back now, I can see that my relationship with my adolescent girl's body was fraught with an underlying threat: When would the next seizure occur? When would my body suddenly throw itself on the floor, and my consciousness disappear—embarrassingly, inconveniently, and painfully?

Avoiding gym classes, playing around in the summertime ocean, doing some body surfing, and climbing the occasional tree—these were my ideas of "sports activities." Until I discovered the meditation of running. Then my world did change. My body and I became more intimate. We glowed. We sweated. We gloried. I'd found not only my sport, but my *practice*.

Like so many back in the early '70s, I was hooked on running. It became a passion, a truly positive addiction. And boy did I get skinny! But this turned out to be the least of the benefits that I experienced. By the time I was running an average of thirty miles a week, my body—that same body that had routinely, unexpectedly, violently betrayed me with every frightening and painful epileptic convulsion—had become a strong, reliable friend. Somehow, I had regained control. I felt empowered.

Running was so easy and so difficult at the same time. Just put on shoes and head out the door. Start slow, get everything going, and then a rhythm would kick in. My breathing, heartbeat, and muscle movements formed a sort of trance dance across whatever surface I was on. In those early years, we didn't know to avoid concrete and tarmac. But I was lucky, living in Vermont. There were always beautiful places—big, dripping trees, sometimes shedding leaves, or rain, or snow crystals. There might be humus underfoot. Or ice.

At the urging of one of my newfound running mates, I tried entering some races—local 5Ks and the like. I quickly ascertained that the competitive aspect of running was not for me. Rather than being a platform to play out the rush for and desire to "win," running afforded me a calming, centering experience. The mind /body synergy, awareness of my breath, sensing and interacting with the natural world— these were the gifts that my daily run bestowed on me. I would come home from a run so energized, my creative juices overflowing and bursting to get out. I didn't know then, either, about the endorphin effect. We knew so little, really, in those early days of the running craze. Magazines came out—*Runner's World*, *Running Times*, and others. Jim Fixx hit the scene in 1977 with his book *The Complete Book of Running*, and we were all so shocked when he died in 1984—running.

If, for some reason, I could not do my daily run, I became grumpy, irascible. While I was still living with my husband, he'd say, "Please, Lisa! Go for your run, would you?" And during those early Jogbra years, with all that travel, I found myself running in some pretty strange places, and often alone. Frankly, when I look back at some of the situations in which I put myself in order to get in a quick run, well, I am in wonder of my younger self.

Running changed me. My energy increased. My creativity felt boundless. My artwork and writing flowed with ease. The strength and power I experienced while running expanded into my everyday life, crept into my attitude, and informed my decision-making. I began to recognize and acknowledge expectations for myself and my life—expectations that I had quietly harbored for many years but never acted upon. I took a big step and officially enrolled in UVM to finish my undergraduate degree.

I also was able to face one of my biggest fears.

I admitted to myself that my marriage of seven years was not working and that my continual attempts to heal it had not been productive. The realization that my marriage had to end was monumental. It meant contemplating the prospect of living alone and becoming self-sufficient for virtually the first time in my life. Marriage for a woman with epilepsy in the '60s and '70s was more than a culmination of a romantic partnership—it was a coping mechanism to deal with a medical dilemma. The reality that my marriage needed to end was frightening. I knew I must use this transition to recreate myself. Though daunting, structuring an unmarried life was, when I could admit it, also an exciting prospect.

I wasn't the only one experiencing upheaval and transition. The year 1977 was pregnant with change and cultural evolution, for women certainly, but also for almost every-one in the boomer generation. Aside from the rumblings of the Women's Movement and the consistent undercur-rent of the Civil Rights Movement, Jimmy Carter had just been elected president of the United States. One of the first things he did as president was to grant a pardon to all the men who had found a way to avoid the military draft for Vietnam—"draft dodgers" they were called at the time. For me and my friends, Carter's pardon was huge. The Vietnam conflict had loomed large in our young adulthood and had been a source of anxiety and concern for our brothers, boy-friends, and husbands. While we were in college, just a few years earlier, we waited to hear status reports on those who were serving, sending them cards and letters. My room-mate lost her older brother there. Young men were being drafted then, and in the late '60s and early '70s, many of those guys graduating were either joining the Peace Corps, praying for 4F medical status, or fleeing to Canada. By 1977, some who'd fled were wondering if they'd ever be able to come home again. I liked Jimmy Carter right away. He seemed to be heralding change, a more forgiving idea of statesmanship.

Around that time, my sister Victoria had also begun jogging—as we referred to running back then. While on the phone together one morning, she started complaining about her breasts bouncing uncomfortably while she ran.

"I can't stand it, Lisa. Do you have any secret or trick? How do you cope?"

"I have no great trick. The only thing I've tried that helps a little bit is to wear a bra with cup sizes that are too small. It reduces the bounce effect somewhat. But every bra feels tight and sweaty around my ribs by the end of my run. And the damn straps stretch out and fall off my shoulders. I'm always having to pull them back up. What a pain!"

"Jeesh! Why isn't there a jockstrap for women?" I could hear the grin in her voice.

"Yeah, same concept, different part of the anatomy!" I concurred. We both laughed.

"A 'jock bra'!" one of us said between the laughter, thoroughly enjoying our familial silliness.

"You know what? I'll do it! I'm gonna make a jockstrap for women—a jock bra!" I declared.

I hung up the phone, dwelling on the conversation and smiling at our repartee. It was true, though, the discomfort of breast movement and my ill-fitting bra were something that could greatly diminish my joy of the run. I grabbed one of my spiral-bound notebooks and a pen, sat right down at the dining-room table, and began to list the attributes of such a bra:

- minimize breast movement
- have straps that wouldn't slip off the shoulders

- no chafing from the seams or clasps
- be made of a light "breathable" fabric to minimize sweating

This "jock bra" idea was taking shape in my mind. As I noodled out my list of attributes, I wondered—could this bra be modest enough, "swim-suity" enough, for me to actually take off my T-shirt while running? Wouldn't that be amazing! The thought was tantalizing. But heaven knows, sewing was not part of my repertoire. I could design and build a stained-glass window from scratch, draw pretty much anything, take shorthand, and type quickly, but I'd practically failed my sewing class in eighth grade. So, of course, I turned to my friend Polly.

What do Miss Piggy and I have in common? Polly.

Polly Smith—my friend since we met in eighth grade at the Kimberley School for Girls in Montclair, New Jersey—had not only passed in our early sewing class, she had excelled in it. In fact, she grew up to become an award-winning costume designer for *The Muppets*! Pardon the pun, but it was a fitting job for her inventive and comic whimsy.

At Kimberley, Polly and I had hung out with the artsy crowd, creating imaginative pranks, avoiding gym classes, getting into a lot of mischief together. During our second year together at school, we fabricated an entire fantasy life. We convinced (we were quite sure) the other girls in our class that our fabrication was real. Only we knew that the letters from, er, England had fake postmarks. Polly had actually carved a rubber stamp in an approximation good enough to fool other fourteen-year-old girls. Or so we thought. Then there were the photos "proving" we hung out with an English rock band called the Beatles. They were really pictures of us standing in front of life-size cardboard cutouts we'd pasted together and cleverly stood up behind us. Our classmates may have been out playing field hockey or giggling about some guy from the local boys' school, but not us. Along with our other two friends, Polly and I were busy in our imaginations.

It is no wonder that Polly went on to earn her undergraduate degree in fine arts and her master's in costume design. By the time the mid-1970s rolled around, she was living in New York City, on her way to becoming a successful and renowned costume designer. She now has seven Emmys on her mantelpiece.

While the "divine Miss P," her Muppet friends, and Jim Henson all had the benefit of years of Polly's sartorial design ingenuity, I had access to her design and sewing talents for only that summer of 1977. Yet, that summer with Polly would change my life forever. For the second summer in a row, Polly had come to Burlington to be the costume designer for the Champlain Shakespeare Festival at UVM's Royall Tyler Theatre. It was a good way for her to get out of New York City for the summer while adding a juicy tidbit to her growing resume. When she'd called to see if she could stay in our spare bedroom for the summer, I'd agreed happily. In my world, Polly meant fun.

When my jock bra sewing challenge presented itself, it seemed natural to turn to Polly for help. I trooped upstairs with my jock bra list in hand, finding her sprawled on my guest-room bed, ensconced in one of Trollope's novels.

"Hey, Pol. I've got a great idea."

She peered over the top of her book expectantly. My "great ideas" typically meant mischief of one sort or another. "What is it?" she asked with false and exaggerated impatience, as if annoyed at being interrupted.

"A jock bra—a bra designed specifically for women to wear while they're running. Will you help me make one? Look, I've got a list here, a sort of—" Her loud groan stopped me short. "What?"

"Lisa, you gotta be kidding." She was clearly not enthusiastic.

"Why? What?"

"Bras are not easy. There's only one thing harder to construct than a bra, and that's a shoe."

A bra is like a shoe? I thought. There was more to this sewing business than I'd anticipated. "Why is a bra so difficult?" I plunked down on the bed next to her.

I should interject here that Polly, like me, had deeply disliked gym class. It was one of the things that had drawn us together all those years ago at Kimberley. She viewed my current passion for running with an amused and skeptical eye. Fashionably thin, Polly's interest in intentional exercise back then was minimal—so, I worried, was her interest in my concept of a jock bra. She had no need for it. And she was a busy boss up at the costume shop and was in the middle of a very good book. Yup, I had some heavy wheedling to do if I wanted to convince Polly to help me out and get involved in this latest scheme.

"Why?" I persisted. "Why is a bra such a tough design problem?" Polly put her book down and sat up, warming to the subject.

"Well, because it's not just about draping fabric on the body. A bra, like a shoe, has to encase a part of the body in a way that supports *and* covers. Bras are not just designed; they are sort of engineered. They've got to perform a certain way. And fitting! Lord, bras are a fitting nightmare. So many sizes! Ribcage and breast size have to be taken into consideration and worked out together, and with that rib-to-boob measurement—forget it!" Polly relaxed down into the bed again, bringing her book back up to her face in an attempt to dismiss me and my latest brainstorm.

Well, I couldn't forget it. I didn't want to forget it. I stayed right there and pressed on, hoping that if I persisted, my new pet project would engage her creative mind. So, annoying friend that I am, I pressed on, playing to the challenge of it all, peppering her with questions and ideas. And really, I was lucky that this jock bra concept was an exciting design problem because, as I'd hoped and suspected, Polly did become drawn into it. Before I left her room, my talented friend and I were huddled over paper, sketching possibilities.

Sketches moved quickly into fabric and findings, with Polly making numerous prototypes based on basic, traditional bra concepts. Each time, I would take Polly's latest engineering feat on a test run, jogging a couple of miles to see how it performed. One cool, summer afternoon, after finishing one such run, I came home and found Polly in the kitchen grabbing a glass of milk.

"How was it?" she asked.

"Miserable! I mean, I had a great run. It's nice today, but this . . ." I snapped the bra strap of the latest jock bra prototype Polly had given me to try, which had inched out from under the neck of my sweaty T-shirt. "This is still not right."

I went into the living room, flopped down on the floor, and folded my torso down over my outstretched legs in a post-run stretch. My nose landed in our sculpted, wall-to-wall, multi-green rug—one of the reasons I loved the apartment. It gave me the illusion of grass, even during Vermont's long, snowy winters. "I am so frustrated," I mumbled into my rug lawn. If this string of design disappointments continued, I was afraid Polly would lose interest in the project. I was aware, too, that wedging in these nontheatrical-related sewing projects up at the theater's costume shop was not easy for her. People were beginning to notice these nonwork-related forays. But despite all this—and the apparent elusiveness of the goal—I was hell-bent on creating a working prototype of my jock bra.

Polly wandered into the living room as I finished stretching out. We were sitting there chatting about jock bra design alternatives, a bit disheartened, when Al came down the stairs and paused on the landing, a couple of steps from the bottom. Always the comedian, he commanded our attention from his latest stage. "Ladies, ladies! Your work is done! Your trials and frustrations are over! I present your jock bra!" There, standing on the stairs, was my six foot four, red-bearded husband with his jockstrap pulled over his head, the waistband tight around his chest, and the strap pulled over his shoulder, causing the pouch to stretch over his chest in a *most* bra-like way.

Polly and I thought we would wee in our pants. The more we laughed, the funnier it seemed. Fully engaged in the comedy and wanting to keep the giggle going, I got up and rushed over to see how this ridiculous jockstrap bra would look on me and my very real 34C breasts. Cramming myself next to him on the landing, I wrestled the jockstrap over Al's head and down over mine. We cackled as I maneuvered and jiggled my right, T-shirted breast into the upside-down jockstrap pouch, pulled one strap over my shoulder, and nudged the waistband down around my ribcage. I hopped off the stairs and started jumping up and down. Polly and Al's laughter reached a new pitch.

For the first few seconds, I didn't even notice that this crazy, jockstrap contraption was actually holding my right breast firmly—that the waistband felt secure, unmovable. Then, suddenly, I did notice, and my demeanor changed instantly. I stopped laughing. Amid Al and Polly's chatter and giggles, I shouted, "I didn't bounce!" They both looked at me oddly, their laughter subsiding. "When I put on the jockstrap, I didn't bounce—or hardly, anyway. It feels right. I'm not kidding. Look! This might be it, Polly. Really. No joke!" Bemused, Polly came over to take a closer look. After some poking, prodding, further examination, and conversation, she concurred. Yes, this upside-down, cattywampus jockstrap contraption just might be a design guide for our jock bra.

The next morning, Polly sent her assistant, Hinda Schreiber, over to the UVM bookstore to buy several jockstraps. I had met Hinda before, while up in the costume shop fooling around with Polly and our jock bra. Hinda had come up from NYU to work for Polly that summer. I remember when Polly introduced us.

"Lisa, this is Hinda, my assistant. She's at NYU, my old alma mater," Polly said. "Hinda, this is my landlady and bane of my existence, Lisa Lindahl . . ."

Hinda, a bright-eyed woman with dark, curling hair cropped close to her head, had become curious about what we were busy doing when the Shakespearean codpieces and gauntlets weren't on the cutting table. She'd watched and asked some questions about our side project. She became enthusiastic about the idea from the moment I'd explained the jock bra concept to her. She got it.

After Polly introduced me to Hinda, I enjoyed and welcomed Hinda's enthusiasm for my idea. A lifelong skier, she had always been encouraged to be athletic and she intuitively got the jock bra concept. Whenever I was up in the costume shop, Hinda would come see where we were at with the jock bra, and I was happy to tell her.

"Isn't there anything like it available now?" she asked me one day.

"Uh, no . . . not that I know of. I've never heard of one or seen one. Of course, I haven't actually looked."

"Well, maybe you should!" Hinda declared in her forthright manner, and Polly looked up from the cutting table.

"That's a good idea," Polly chimed in. "We could go down to . . . What's that lingerie store in town?"

"Bertha Church! Of course!" I said.

"At the very least, I could get some construction ideas for this stupid prototype!" Polly continued, waving a triangle of flimsy cloth in my direction.

"I could come along and take notes for you two!" Hinda exclaimed. Polly and I looked at each other and nodded

with that silent, "Why not?" sort of shrug that people sometimes do.

"Okay! Let's go!" And I think we three packed up our
stuff right that moment and trooped off down the hill to
Burlington's main street, Church Street, where the Bertha
Church lingerie store stood. It had been there for years
(and still is to this very day).

It was the sort of retail establishment that sought to
lend decorum to the delicate task of selling ladies undergarments. Quiet, muted colors. Discreet sales displays. Older
saleswomen. And it thrived. So in we went, a three-pronged
burst of noisy energy. At first the elderly saleswoman was
a bit taken aback, but we won her over when I explained
our mission.

"Well, there is a bra for tennis," she declared, moving
toward one of her inventory drawers. I recall having a moment of real panic, tinged with disappointment. Had my
idea already been taken? But then she brought it out and I
went into a dressing room and tried it on. It was simply a
regular bra, though very white.

"This isn't different at all! What makes it especially for
tennis?" I asked the woman.

"I don't know. The name?" she responded. I was relieved and energized anew in my pursuit to create a true
bra for runners.

"What else do you have?" asked Polly. And thus ensued
a rather hilarious hour in Bertha Church's fitting room,

with me trying on many different bras and jogging in place, while Polly inspected every mode of closure, elastic, and type of fabric. We clucked over useless garnishes and ridiculous straps. Hinda stood just outside the curtain, trying to take notes.

We left the store, fatigued but assured that there was no bra currently on the market that could be comfortably worn while a woman was being active. It was a rather startling confirmation, really. Sometime after this outing—karmic wheel turning, turning—I asked Polly if she would mind if I asked Hinda to "officially" help us on the jock bra project. I wanted, I think, Hinda's enthusiastic energy in the mix.

My first impression of Hinda was that here, perhaps, was a true kindred spirit. Athletic and amply bosomed, I felt she was perhaps more simpatico than Polly about the idea of and need for a running bra. When I learned she was a vegetarian, skier, part-time yoga instructor, and interested in the work of one of the Indian gurus of the time, I assumed she shared my "New Age" values. Also, getting Polly to help me create a bra for jogging hadn't been so easy. She was intrigued by the design challenge and wanted to support me (pun intended), but I feared her interest may not go much further. And I knew myself well enough to know that I preferred working with others versus working solo. So I remember asking Polly if it would be okay if I invited enthusiastic Hinda to work with us on the jock bra.

Polly—feeling Hinda didn't know a lot of people in the area and might be somewhat lonely—agreed.

And so, I invited Hinda in.

After procuring the jockstraps, Polly cut up two of them—snipping here, reassembling there—and *presto!* The new prototype emerged. That evening, after she had finished her workday at Royall Tyler Theatre, Polly walked down the hill to my house and presented me with the Frankenstein-esque item. Hinda joined us, and with much giggling and renewed optimism, I pulled this latest and weirdest prototype over my head. It was time for yet another test run.

"I'll run backward in front of you to see if you bounce!" Hinda declared. And, as has been reported in the press ever since, she did. For a few blocks, Hinda jogged in front of me, backward, watching to see how much my breasts appeared to bounce as I ran in the two sewn-together jockstraps. It was clear almost immediately that *this* prototype was working.

The materials used in jockstraps were, we agreed, awful. Sure, we now had the overall design concept, but before a truly accurate sewing pattern could be determined, we needed to know what fabrics and elastics would be right for our jock bra. Was there a soft, plush-backed elastic wide enough to perform as a rib band? What would work for the cup area? For the straps? It was another puzzle for Polly's creative design mind.

Polly had been offered a job designing an off-Broadway play, a big deal at that point in her career. The people at the Royall Tyler were impressed as well and allowed her a break to go down to New York to get that project rolling. She had designed the last Shakespeare play of their season and could leave Hinda in charge. We agreed that while Polly was in New York she should take the opportunity to find the right fabrics and elastics for our jock bra. Thus, it was during this trip that Polly made the creative and critical recommendation to use the new, and as yet unheard of, cotton Lycra fabric for the cup section. She also found a plush-lined, two-inch elastic for the rib band and a one-inch elastic for the straps and set to work. When she came back up to Vermont, she had a pattern, complete with a true, working jock bra prototype in my size. I went running in it and was elated.

The rest, as they say, is history.

2.

STARTING LINES

"If at first you don't succeed, try, try again!"
~ *Thomas H. Palmer*

As the summer of 1977 ended, we all had to go back to our "real lives." Polly returned to New York City to begin the next phase of her costume-designing career with that off-Broadway play, and Hinda went off to teach costume design at the University of South Carolina.

But before they left, I called the three of us together for a chat on my living-room floor. What next? We now had a prototype of the jock bra, but what now? What did they think? I was coming at the prospect from a sew-it-and-sell-it viewpoint. Having spent the previous few years augmenting my income on the craft-fair circuit with my stained-glass windows and lampshades, I was envisioning a variation of that theme. Only in this case, I wouldn't be doing the making. I'd heard of "cottage industries," so I was thinking we'd be able to employ a lot of women in their homes to make our jock bras. It could be a real women-for-women enterprise!

I'd figure out where to place ads with order coupons. We could have a nice little mail-order business on the side. For me, the income could help pay for my graduate school, and there would be no driving—a bonus for someone without a license.

Well, Polly correctly shot down the cottage industry idea in a nanosecond. She knew that world much better than I did. She informed me on two points: first, quality control in any sort of cottage industry involving sewing was difficult, and secondly, and most importantly, the jock bra was an extremely difficult product to sew together because it was attaching stretch fabrics onto stretch fabrics—an art requiring expertise that was not readily found in home sewers. And she talked a lot about sewing-related things that at the time I wasn't able to fully appreciate.

We then talked of buying sewing machines and hiring sewers—a complicated and intimidating prospect. Finding an existing sewing house? Polly spoke up again, telling horror stories of some of the sweatshops she had seen in her years of working her way through school. We brainstormed other alternatives. If we weren't going to make the product ourselves, how might we get the jock bra out to market? In essence we were blue-skying.

It was evident to me that going forward was going to be complicated. In that conversation there on my grass-like living-room floor, we could not settle on the how, exactly, but we spoke quite a bit about other things—like philosophy and how we could create something beyond just the product, a different sort of entity. We were friends working together, trying to bring a needed product to market, creating our own financial stability. Being independent women, trusting and relying on one another—giving mutual support—yes! Well, it was 1977, after all.

So, without coming to any real action plan, but with lots of hugs and a vision, off Polly and Hinda went on their separate ways. Me, well, I'd never really left my "real life." The finished prototype was in my hands. School, work, running, art, a marriage, and the jock bra were all still there to claim my time and concern when autumn hit Vermont.

I grew up in the '60s, a transformational decade of change and volatility. The Civil Rights Movement was well underway; there were marches and sit-ins. I remember going on a bus from New Jersey down to Washington, DC to join a protest. Birth control was new and "free love" was busy undermining all us "good girls" who had been taught to define success as marriage and a family. In the two-year women's college that I graduated from in 1968, a required course was "Marriage and the Family"—I kid you not. But the old societal rules were disintegrating, and my generation of women knew it. We were growing up without the predictability that had been both comforting and oppressive for our mothers. It was the "Age of Aquarius"—our skirts got short, everybody's hair got long, Simon & Garfunkel were singing "Bridge Over Troubled Water," and the pursuit of "higher consciousness" kicked in. For some, that involved drugs.

I recall writing to my neurologist from my college dorm room. I had been told to never drink alcohol because of my epilepsy medications. I wrote to him, depending upon doctor-patient confidentiality, saying that alcohol was not a risk (I didn't like the taste) but that I needed to know his medical opinion, please, about this other stuff—marijuana, specifically. Was smoking marijuana dangerous for a person with epilepsy? He wrote back saying only that it was illegal. *So* helpful, and not new information. But this memory is another indicator: it was a changing and different time. I hadn't dared ask him about other things floating around in the dorm rooms. I got through, though, exploring my options and expanding my consciousness without the aid of anything more mind-expanding than a very occasional shared joint. It was in the party situations back then that I learned to say, with a genuine laugh, "Hey, I take drugs so I *don't* hallucinate." And I wasn't kidding, as any person who has experienced seizures and the accompanying altered state, called an "aura," can tell you.

But my college education had been interrupted, first by some financial hurdles and then by my choice to marry. These had put me on another path, so I found it very rewarding to have finally gone back to finish college and find that I loved it—and that I did well in my classes. I was even eyeing continuing on to graduate school at UVM. Pursuing art in my makeshift studio in the basement had taken a definite back seat. Dust covered my worktable and tools. Running, of course, was still a daily devotion and discipline. Through the act of running, I was becoming a much stronger, happier woman.

That nascent self-confidence was not only allowing me to begin to face the facts about my marriage, but also to start challenging many old, ingrained limitations that had held me back in the past. I don't believe that I would have had the guts to go back to undergraduate school, as a married, working, "older" woman, had I not started running. Believe it or not, such a thing was unusual at that time.

My inner landscape was shifting, just as the outside world of the 1970s was shifting. A few of my classes were in the new area of "women's studies." It was an era now referred to as "second wave feminism," when NOW (National Organization for Women) was pushing the Equal Rights Amendment and *Ms.* magazine, Simone De Beauvoir, and Betty Friedan—not to mention the essay "The Personal Is Political" by Carol Hanisch—all made every thinking woman review her choices and decisions. It was a time of long discussions over late-night coffees. It was a time that was both confusing and fertile. It was a time pregnant with change.

The jock bra had been my idea. It was my baby. I had first enlisted Polly to help me create a physical prototype, and then Hinda. It seemed natural and appropriate to all of us that, having achieved that end, the next move was left up to me. So in that September of 1977, I pondered the steps necessary to create a business around the bra. Polly had sourced the right fabrics and elastics in New York, so we now had a complete and working prototype. To move things forward, I had a lot of research to do—both of the practical and soul-searching variety. And in our summer's-end conversation, Polly had made it quite clear that we did not want to be sewing our own bras—so what were our options?

I had a vague notion that we might sell this product to some "big company." And I knew I would have to research how to make this happen. But I had a basic question about this direction: If the bra was to be sold to an existing and established company, who was selling it? Me? What about Polly, who'd actually overcome the design challenges and translated the idea into cloth and elastic? And if Polly, what about Hinda, who had shown enthusiasm and encouragement? And who, I suspected, would continue to do so.

Al and I had a friend who was an attorney, so I gave him a call. Bob had a well-appointed office in downtown Burlington. On one of the first brisk autumn days, I walked down the College Street hill to his office. I was nervous, entering territory about which I knew very little. I'm guessing I adopted my "student" attitude.

Bob took the time to explain the phenomenon of corporations to me. I thought I understood. After speaking to him, I came to the decision that I would form a corporate entity, giving Polly and Hinda shares. This way, our little company—not just me—could sell the jock bra to some big company, and we all would get a little something for our summertime endeavor. I came up with a name—SLS Inc., denoting the initials of our three last names, Smith, Lindahl and Schreiber.

I remember distinctly a conversation I had with Al at this juncture. After our attorney friend had explained the concept of "shares," he asked me how many shares would go to whom. He assumed that I, as the project lead and president of the newly incorporated SLS Inc., would have the most shares—and therefore control. Remember, though, this was the '70s, and I was a partial product of the '60s. I was a sometime hippie, lifelong artist, and nascent feminist who touted peace and love for all beings. So it was really inevitable that the nature of control, of power, of being "in power," would come up in my discussion with Al about incorporating and this concept of share division.

Did I say Al's graduate degree was a master's in divinity and that he worked in social services? True. "If you all have equal shares, there can be no power trips," Al advised,

"everyone will have equal authority—a true partnership!"
And this resonated with me.

Hey, in the '70s, in the groups we traveled with, "power
tripping" was on a par with farting at the dinner table. Not
only was it disgusting, it was unenlightened. Old-school,
dominator culture behavior. Not cool. It revealed a weak,
greedy character. This was the time of Martin Luther King,
Jr., Nixon, Watergate, and Take Back the Night marches
were occurring in cities all over the country. So, idealisti-
cally and altruistically, trusting in my fledgling, feminist
vision, I made what would turn out to be a pivotal decision.
After incorporating in that October of 1977, I would create
shares and divide them equally among us three, sending
Hinda and Polly equal shares: one-third, one-third, one-
third. In return, I would ask each of them to send me $100
to "pay" for their shares. At least I'd have some money to
cover Bob's fees for drawing up the incorporation papers.
Although I acquiesced to Bob's strong suggestion to make
myself the corporation's president, I was determined to
issue the shares in equal portions. In my mind, it was necessary to our "for women, by women" business model. I don't
think I knew the term "corporate culture" at that point—it
was just something I felt.

Bob drew up the paperwork and issued the shares.
Probably because of what would occur almost a year later,
I have a memory that he did so with an attitudinal shrug,
a sort of condescension that I had learned, over the years,

to ignore. I should not have. Because as it turned out, important safeguards were not in place, and this would come back around to trip me up...big time.

I took the $100 they had each sent me and opened a corporate checking account. Our first check went to Bob. I then took out all the interest that had accumulated in my personal savings account and added it to the pot as well. This made my contribution greater than Polly's or Hinda's—if only minimally. Truth is, in the beginning, I knew I was more invested in the project than either of them, so it seemed fitting. Hell, they weren't even around anymore.

With little professional experience, and a lot of determination and native curiosity, I began a series of frustrating and confusing queries into the world of business. I kept thinking that the most efficacious way to proceed would be to structure some sort of deal with a large company. I had heard of licensing but didn't have a clue as to what it might entail.

I bemoaned the fact that I could not turn to my father for help. Brilliant in business, especially marketing, it was said of him that whatever company he worked for, the stock went up. But he had suffered a debilitating stroke just two years earlier. The powerful presence of my childhood was now a maudlin old man in a wheelchair. I saw him only on my brief trips back to my parents' home in New Jersey, and he wasn't able to speak well enough for us to really communicate. I don't know how much he really understood about what I was trying to do.

For advice and guidance, I turned to the only person I knew well then in the for-profit business world—my sister's husband, Dick, who had been in sales in a major corporation for more than a decade. At my request, Dick talked to the corporate lawyers at his company about licensing, how to get a patent, and what precautions should be taken. In my telephone discussions with Dick, it became very clear that there were significant risks for an inventor trying to sell an unprotected product, especially a garment, to a large company. Although I was in the process of trademarking the jock bra name, I had been unable to find a lawyer in Vermont who could do the patent work. I was also learning that garments rarely received patents because such patents were too easy to break. Garments were not considered technically complicated or unique. You need only change a seam or a thread specification and suddenly it's a different garment.

By early November, I was a bit discouraged. I didn't know what avenue to take and felt at a loss as to what the next step should be to turn my idea into a reality. Then, one bright autumnal morning, my phone rang. It was Dick, saying he thought he'd found the answer to "our" problems. His tone and pronoun use told me he was beginning to feel attached to the project. It seemed he had found a company called World Inventors Inc. that claimed to take care of all aspects of taking an invention to market. From soup (R&D, the patent) to nuts (sales and marketing).

Dick forwarded the company's brochure to me. Indeed, it seemed to promise the very world. "We'll present your idea to the people that can make it happen," the brochure proclaimed, without much hard information about how they would do it. They had what appeared to me to be an elaborate fee structure. We needed to send in $250 with our signed contract, then more than $1,000 to "package your idea," and then something like another $3,000 to take it out to the world. In 1977, this was a great deal of money to me. But Dick was enthusiastic. He even said he was willing to help pay the initial sign-on fee.

But something didn't feel right to me about World Inventors. I didn't know how to articulate it. I hadn't seen their contract, so I didn't have anything substantial on which to base my sense of unease. Dick and I agreed to look at the contract and discuss it further when we saw each other at a family gathering on Thanksgiving. In the ensuing weeks, however, I came to a decision on a course of action. Since I didn't know what else to do, and Dick believed in this group's spiel enough to front some money, I decided I would tell him at Thanksgiving that I was willing to take a shot with these guys, providing, of course, that their contract seemed reasonable. Something or someone had to move this project forward. Polly was enmeshed in her work in New York City and Hinda had disappeared to the South to teach. They were living their "real lives," and I did not fault them for it. It was my responsibility—now with Dick's help—to move this entrepreneurial experiment to the next level.

Thanksgiving approached and I went down to Pennsylvania to my Aunt Lucy's holiday gathering. She and Uncle Fran lived in a large, comfortable home nestled in Bucks County. I hadn't been to Thanksgiving at my aunt's since I was a teen, and I was newly struck with the beauty of the place. The countryside seemed like a softer, somehow more refined version of where I lived in Vermont. I was happy to be there. I was full of anticipation and excitement, busy regaling distant relatives with tales of the jock bra invention.

After filling ourselves with turkey, scalloped oysters, mashed potatoes, yams, turnips, and chestnut stuffing, we all needed to go for a walk. My aunt and uncle located coats and scarves. Several cousins, my brother, some others, and I stepped out into the brisk November gloaming. The dark hills were misted with gray, and here and there a few defiant leaves still clung to branches, crackling in the light wind. Dick came up beside me, matching his step to mine. From his breast pocket he pulled out a folded document and handed it to me. I took it in my gloved hand and smiled up at him. I was sure he was handing me the contract from World Inventors, so I could review it and sign. It was a big moment, a big step forward. I unfolded the pages, noting that there were several. Coming upon the last page, I stopped walking. Standing there, I blinked and concentrated, looking again at that last page. It looked like I was holding an executed document. The light was dim, so I looked more closely. Yes, there was definitely a signature. There, in the space designated for the inventor's signature, my brother-in-law Dick had signed his name.

I remember feeling like time had stopped on that chilly day in Bucks County. I became very aware of my surroundings, noting the thick hem of bare, brown trees lining the rural road on both sides of us. Was it time for little Lisa to grow up? Oh, I hated this! I looked at the threatening gray clouds on the horizon, took a deep breath, and resumed walking, quickly now. Dick had kept walking on ahead, and when I caught up to him, I blurted, "Dick! How could you sign for me? You're not the inventor. I haven't agreed to this contract." Even as the words left my lips, I felt guilty for not trusting my brother-in-law's intentions.

He explained that World Inventors was pressuring "us" to make a commitment, so he'd seen no harm in his signing the contract. He told me he'd even sent them his personal check for $250 along with the contract.

I kept stuttering things like, "But I'm the inventor!" and "I'm the President of SLS!" Angry and flustered, I was unable to articulate in the moment what I knew to be true:

he had no authority, legally or morally, to sign that piece of paper. He was either very naïve or trying to manipulate the situation in what felt like an underhanded way. Either way, it didn't feel good or right. It was clear he thought he was doing me a favor. His indignant response made that apparent. And he couldn't conceal his anger about my reaction. Once again, I felt like the little girl who was not being taken seriously—for whom others "knew best." It had been a constant theme in my life as a person with epilepsy. This time, I was not going to swallow that pill. We ended the walk in a bitter argument, rife with accusations.

Indigestion became the result of that Thanksgiving of 1977. When I got back to Vermont, I sent Dick a check to pay back his $250. I then phoned World Inventors, apprising them of the situation and nullifying the contract. It wasn't until several years later that Dick and I felt comfortable with each other again. Needless to say, that was the end of any future with World Inventors Inc.—and almost the end of my relationship with my brother-in-law.

After the holidays, I began the spring semester at UVM. I had decided to use my fledgling bra business as a case study in the systems class I needed for my master's degree. Beyond that, I didn't have much intellectual, emotional, or monetary coin to put into the jock bra project. This was due in large part to the fact that, as 1978 dawned, I was finally, actively confronting Al and discussing with him the possibility and the hows of ending our marriage of seven and a half years—and I was extremely frightened of what that might mean.

The first step, a physical separation, meant living alone, and this created a number of medical and logistical issues for me. My primary epilepsy fear was having a major seizure event *alone*. "Alone" translated into a higher probability of ill effects—like injury or death. If that sounds dramatic, understand that this had been drummed into me by every doctor and reinforced by family members ever since the epilepsy had escalated from the short-absence seizures of my childhood into the full-blown convulsions that blossomed in my adolescence. The biggest logistical complication, of course, was my lack of a driver's license and my perception that I was unable to get one in Vermont.

My husband and I, in our let's-try-this-out, newly separated status, were trading off weeks living in our apartment during that spring of 1978. He lived in a motel when not in the apartment, and when it was his turn to have the apartment, I stayed with a friend a few blocks away. It was a stressful time. I was concerned that the one-and-only prototype of the jock bra (now on its way to becoming a product name, "Jock Bra") could get mislaid amid the general confusion—both logistical and emotional. I was also feeling that, aside from birthing the idea itself, I had done a lot of work to set up the corporation, explore the trademark process, and research how to license or sell the idea to an existing company. Not to mention the World Inventors disaster. So, I thought it was one of my partners' turns to take a whack at getting us to the next step.

My choice in this matter was Hinda, for two reasons: First, Polly had helped me with the initial design work. She'd gone to New York and sourced the fabric and elastic that would make that design work, and then she'd whipped up our actual prototype. Second, while Hinda was more overtly enthusiastic than Polly, she had not yet really *done* anything to warrant her ownership. So, I sent the prototype down to Hinda in South Carolina. I remember calling her and telling her that my marriage was falling apart, that I wasn't even sure where I'd be living in the coming months, and that I needed help with the jock bra project. Could she please keep the prototype safe and take a stab at exploring next steps?

It was a step that would change the course of the company in more than one way.

3.

BREASTS AND OUR DIVINE FEMININITY

"My mission in life is not merely to survive, but to thrive; and to do so with some passion, some compassion, some humor, and some style."
~ *Maya Angelou*

For me, this "Jock Bra" was simply a solution to my own problem. And then I thought, well, if I want it, I bet other women will, too. In making it available to others, I was also able to solve my own employment problem—because the product was successful from the instant it went on the market. Building the company was a wild, ever-changing ride. But while on it, I never had any idea that my invention would become as significant as it has proven to be. I really had no idea that there were so many other girls and young women out there who were too embarrassed or afraid to walk out on the field, the court, or the gym floor because of the issues they were having with their breasts.

We all know, ladies, that growing breasts is an ongoing relationship. They don't just pop out, we say "hello," and then go about our business as if "that's done!"—as if nothing has changed. So much has changed, is changing! On the breast front alone: They bud. They swell. They hurt. They get too big . . . or not big enough. Then, our clothes fit differently. We have to buy a bra, or bras, and figure all that out. And when the breasts are all done appearing, suddenly we start getting paid a new type of attention that wasn't there before. And then we have to manage *that*. To top it off, every month, the girls may decide to get tender... or not. We won't even go into the lactating-breast adventures for those who choose to have children; they are too myriad. Finally, as we age, they begin to sag. And our clothes fit differently, again. Oh yes, women are in a relationship with their breasts. This is not a new or modern phenomenon. There is a long history here, and it has nothing to do with men or the male gaze.

Our breasts are a manifestation of our power, our unique attributes, our fertility, and our ability to feed our young. But as women have always known—from the single-breasted Amazonians to the World Cup–winning female soccer players—when it comes to being active, to being athletic, our relationship with our breasts can suddenly come to the forefront in a whole new way. I was just another participant in my relationship with my breasts during the cultural tumult of the late twentieth century. The important bit is that I listened to my intuition and, in acting upon it, enlisted help in the areas that I needed it.

4.

OFF AND RUNNING

"When I let go of what I am, I become what I might be."
~ Lao Tzu

When the summer of 1978 rolled around, my life was beginning to reflect all the changes that had been brewing for some time. Old patterns were dissolving, and new people—classmates, my professors up at UVM—were appearing. After months of an on-again, off-again marriage during our trial separation—and all the drama that entailed—Al permanently moved out of our apartment that August.

I was grateful that I was the one who was able to stay. That place was home to me. Even as my safety-blanket marriage was failing, I was aware that I could not face going forward alone without that lovely space and the gardens I'd planted outside—both surrounded me in beauty, serenity, and security. I felt safe there. This was made absolutely real to me the time I had a convulsion while standing on the top landing of the stairs. I lost consciousness before falling.

Somehow, however, I had the knowingness, the familiarity of place, to fall *upward*, rather than down the stairs. I didn't break my neck. I believe that it was my relationship with the place that allowed this to happen, that safeguarded me in that instance.

It doesn't do it justice to refer to 359 College Street as an apartment. Really, it was more like a town house—the rear ell section of a big old house, built circa 1800s, that had been sectioned off and made into a two-story, separate living space. It stood on its elegant green lawn midway down the hill that led from the old redbrick buildings of the university at the top and down to the center of the town on the edge of Lake Champlain at the bottom.

My part was probably once the kitchen, back stairs, and two bedrooms of the main house, now transformed into my living room, dining room, kitchen, and back porch downstairs, and upstairs were two bedrooms and a bath. The plentiful double-hung windows were large and some of the windowpanes still had the old, wavy glass in them. My windows faced north and south. I got great light.

Although still legally married, I was experiencing and confronting the practical aspects of living alone. In preparation for what my future now seemed to promise, Al—nice person that he was—had taught me how to drive. I had researched what I needed to do to get a driver's license in Vermont, and I was putting in extra hours at a work-study position I'd secured up at UVM. I was, most definitely, having a growth spurt of the personal variety.

I completed all my undergrad credit requirements and did not miss a beat. I began taking a lot of graduate courses. I'd crafted and received preliminary approval on my individually designed major for the M.Ed. program and was excited about pursuing it. And, of course, I hoped that the jock bra business might eventually bring in a little something once I'd figured that scene out. Between attending classes and doing homework, going to my "Susie Secretary" work, running every day, and finding my way into a new lifestyle, I was a tad occupied. I took some of my calligraphy pens, hand-lettered a sign, and hung it over my big, old oak desk at home where I paid bills and did homework. It said simply, "PERSEVERE"—all in elegant caps. Life for me, at that moment in time, was overflowing with responsibilities and possibilities—frightening *and* exhilarating.

After Hinda received the prototype, she started showing it around to local sporting goods stores in Columbia, South Carolina. One woman she called on told her that "jock" was not considered a nice word in the South and suggested we reconsider the name for our piece of athletic equipment for the breasts. It had never occurred to us that a jock meant anything other than someone who was seriously into sports, although it did have a definite male connotation.

I actually thought that might make the name catchier and more memorable.

I remember the phone call from Hinda. "The 'Jock Bra' name isn't going to work. 'Jock' isn't a word that would be used in polite company, is what I've been told." She seemed in a bit of a panic. "But then, I mean, really Lisa, does it even matter . . . *really*?"

I thought for a minute. "I think it does. We can't afford to turn off a whole region of the country. And whaddaya know, Hinda, maybe there are other areas, other people that feel the same way?" What I was actually thinking was "Better safe than sorry!" Besides, another name was forming in my mind.

"What the hell are we going to do now? What are we going to call the Jock Bra?" Hinda wondered over the phone.

"*Jogbra*. We'll call it the Jogbra! All one word! A new word! It is for jogging, after all!" So it was decided, and the Jogbra was born.

And then Hinda did a marvelous thing. Sometime that summer, she was successful in locating a small factory outside Columbia to produce our newly christened Jogbra. South Carolina has a long history with the textile industry. Production of textiles had existed there at one level or another from shortly after the Revolutionary War right up until the end of the twentieth century. In the late 1970s, there were still massive, active brick mills. In the smaller towns in the Piedmont area, near Greenville, South

Carolina, entire communities might rely on a mill for their livelihoods. Generations of entire families had grown up working for particular factories. But the industry was declining, and people were losing their jobs.

Hinda had come across a couple, JD and Caroline, who had each probably worked in one of those big mills. They had struck out on their own in Columbia, wanting to start their own clothing-manufacturing facility. JD was a machinist who could fix anything that might go wrong with a sewing machine. Caroline could cut and sew and run a sewing line. Budding entrepreneur to budding entrepreneurs, they worked out how the Jogbra might be mass-produced for a reasonable unit cost. Eager to start their own operation, this couple was willing and able to do the very small production runs we needed initially for the Jogbra. This was serendipitous indeed. An established factory would not have had anything to do with a start-up or a one-product company offering only a small, unpredictable production schedule.

Go-ahead girl that she was, Hinda borrowed $5,000 from her father to buy raw materials (fabric, elastic, etc.) and have JD and Caroline do a sample production run. I learned this when she sent his check to me to deposit into the business checking account I'd set up when I'd formed the corporation, along with instructions that I should expect to see bills from some fabric suppliers coming in and to please pay them. So began our partnership with Active

Manufacturing, as JD and Caroline had named their new enterprise. Both companies began, then, in earnest, together.

Finally, we were going to have some bras to sell. But where were women going to actually buy our Jogbra? That's what I started thinking about next.

Today, women may take for granted that they can walk into a sporting goods store or visit an online retailer and buy a sports bra. But back in the '70s, bras were only sold in two places: department stores and lingerie specialty stores. From the little I knew from talking with my brother-in-law and a few friends, the lingerie and department store businesses were cutthroat and full of old, dyed-in-the-wool players. Remember, this was way before the internet. Nonetheless, if I had done any true market research, I probably would have scrapped the whole project. Why? Because that research would have revealed that the bra market had been shrinking for at least the past decade, probably longer.

In that decade, women were burning their bras, if not always literally, then certainly metaphorically. We were the baby-boomer feminists. We deliberately rejected the stockings, girdles, and garter belts our mothers had given our fourteen-year-old selves, and we weren't big on bras either. All the long-established bra companies of the day—Vanity Fair™, Playtex™, Maidenform™—were just fighting for market share. You had to be crazy to start a new bra business.

It was crystal clear that a small entity like Jogbra would not be able to enter the department store and specialty-lingerie market. Somewhere in my queries, researching, or being a nosy pest, I had learned that the department store buying and buyers' culture was steeped in tradition—a sophisticated world of discounting, terms, and quantities. I instinctively knew it was not for us in our fledgling state. A one-product entrepreneurial start-up would not be taken seriously. This bra I'd come up with had helped me on my runs, ergo, I deducted, it was *athletic equipment*. All I needed—all any woman runner needed— was the right shoes and her bra. And where did she buy those running shoes? In a sporting goods store. That's where she could buy her bra, too. And sporting goods outlets were a lot more approachable than department stores.

Ironically, I had never been in a sporting goods store until I had to buy running shoes. Even then, I didn't hang around. They brought back feelings of intimidation from those long-ago gym classes of my childhood, but even more so. To me, sporting goods stores were rank with the culture of competition, something with which I wasn't comfortable. Every time I went into a sporting goods store, I felt I was in a totally alien environment. I also knew that sporting goods stores were often owned or managed by runners. They were referred to as "participant owners." And they were much more approachable than the old-retail guard. So, I overcame my discomfort, and *voilà*—made what turned out to be a brilliant marketing decision: the Jogbra would be sold in sporting goods stores.

The introduction of a sports bra into the bra market resulted in growth of both units and sales revenue. Eventually, every bra manufacturer would have their own version, increasing brassiere sales substantially. Today the sports bra market alone tops $19 billion. Not to mention that the sports bra is credited with being the seed garment for the entire, now booming "athleisure" look and industry.

"Oh, by the way," Hinda phoned to let me know one overcast, summer day, "the sample run is ready. JD and Caroline—y'know, the owners of Active Manufacturing—are shipping them to your apartment."

"To College Street? To my apartment?" I asked, just to confirm. I was taken by surprise. She went on to tell me she had placed an ad in *Running Times* magazine for the Jogbra—and had listed my home telephone number and address in it.

"Uh . . . but wait! You already put this ad in the magazine?"

"Yup."

"With *my* address!? Why my address?" I was trying to digest the news that my personal info was being published in a national magazine and wondering what my very private-minded landlady might think as well. I was once again so grateful that Al and I had agreed I should stay in the apartment while he made other living arrangements. All this flashed across my mind in nanoseconds. I was just plain astonished at Hinda's news, really.

"Because I'm leaving South Carolina. Polly's New York apartment is too small. Your house works best. Let me read you the ad. 'Jogbra—First bra designed just for running! Available now. Dealer inquiries invited!' Then, your Vermont address and telephone number appear."

"What's a dealer? Is that the same as a store, a retailer?"

"Oh, Lisa, I dunno. The guy from the Phidippides store here told me to put it in. So, I did!"

I gulped. What the heck was she thinking? What was a dealer? *My own phone number in a magazine?*

"Oh! And we have to have 'terms.' Y'know, to sell to stores—sales terms. The Phidippides guy told me that, too. He asked me if our terms were 2/10 net 30, and I said yes, because I didn't know, and I didn't want him to know I had no idea what he was talking about."

"2/10 net 30? What does that even mean?" My brain was spinning.

"I didn't know either," Hinda explained. "So, I called over to the biz department at the college here. A prof explained it to me: if they pay us within ten days, then 2 percent off their total bill, but they have to pay us within thirty days and then the whole amount!"

The memory of this conversation, the sweet naïveté of it all, makes me smile now. I was impressed with how quickly Hinda was moving things along—so yeah, all right, of course my address could be in there. *Okay*, I was thinking, *I can adjust to this.* And I glanced up at the reminder over my desk in the living room: *"PERSEVERE!"*

5.

MY LIFELONG PARTNER

"The only disability in life is a bad attitude."
~ Scott Hamilton

L et me tell you a bit about my old friend, epilepsy. Having epilepsy does not make any sort of money-making endeavor easy or reliable, yet it is my other "partner" in life. Husbands, friends and business partners have come and gone, but epilepsy has always been with me. It was my first experience of having a "shadow teacher."

While a child who doesn't feel she has power over her world may have a tantrum, as we grow older most of us find other, more subtle ways to express our powerfulness or powerlessness. We adapt, learn coping mechanisms—how to persuade, manipulate, or capitulate when necessary. These tools, these learned adaptations, give a sense of control. They make us feel more in charge of our destiny. As a result, our maturing self generally feels indestructible, immortal. Life is a long, golden road of futures for the young.

This was not the case for me. I learned very early on, when I started having seizures, that I was not fully in charge of the world, my world, specifically of my body. There are many different types of epileptic seizures. Often a person with the illness may have more than one type. That has been the case for me. I was diagnosed with epilepsy—with a seizure type now referred to as "absence seizures"—when I was four years old. I have seen neurologists and taken medications ever since. As often happens, the condition worsened when I entered puberty, and I started having convulsions as well—what most people think of when they think of epileptic seizures. The clinical name is generalized "tonic-clonic" seizures.

In such a seizure, the entire brain is involved, rather like an electrical circuit that has gone out as a result of a power surge. I lose consciousness, my whole body becomes rigid, my muscles start jerking uncontrollably, and I fall. Tonic-clonic seizures, also known as "grand mal" seizures, may or may not be preceded by an aura, a type of perceptual disturbance, which for me can act as a warning of what is coming. The seizure usually only lasts for a few minutes, but I feel its draining effects for a day or two afterward. Although I would prefer to sleep all day after such a physically and emotionally taxing event, I have often just gotten up off the floor and, within hours, gone back to work. It was necessary sometimes, though definitely not medically advised. I'm fond of saying that having a grand mal seizure is rather like being struck by a Mack truck and living to tell the tale.

Having epilepsy has forced me to be dependent on others throughout my life. While we are all dependent upon others to some degree—independent, interdependent, dependent—in my case, a deep level of dependency was decreed and ingrained very early on. This enforced dependency did not sit well with my native self. I bucked and rebelled. At the same time, a part of me also feared the next fall, the next post convulsive fugue. And so, I recognized, I acquiesced to the need to depend on others.

The silver lining of having epilepsy is that it has introduced me to and taught me a bit about the nature of being powerless—and experiencing betrayal. I could not trust that my body would always operate as it should. Routinely, it suddenly quits. I experience this as betrayal by my brain and body. It results in my complete powerlessness throughout the convulsion. Not to mention an inconvenient interruption of any activities or plans I might have made.

Hence, I am the recipient of two important life lessons—and I was blessed to have this very specific and graphic experience at a young age. It made me observant and reflective, giving me the opportunity to consider what, where, and who "I" was. I knew I was not "just" my body, or even my brain.

So, who or what did that leave? Who or what am I? Much has been written about trauma, and about near-death experiences, both of which seizures have been classified or described as. I won't delve into that here except to say that experiencing recurrent seizures and the attendant altered states of consciousness that sometimes accompany an episode (the euphemism for a seizure) changes you. It deeply affects you. It is both illuminating and frightening. It opens you up in some ways and can close you way down in others. For me, it made it easy to consider the possibility of other ways to perceive, the possibility of other realms. And as an adult, I became interested in quantum physics, where science is pushing and challenging our long-held perceptual assumptions. Me, who was poor in math and disinterested in science while in school! So if not merely body and brain, who am I? Spirit. And with epilepsy's tutelage, I was encouraged to question, seek, and try to understand what lies beyond.

Living with epilepsy has also given me great strength. In realizing the futile nature of trying to have "power over" epilepsy, I developed a deep well of "power within"—that inner strength that comes with the acceptance of that which one cannot change—and looking beyond it.

Through my experience building the Jogbra business, with the unique lens afforded me by my epilepsy partner, I came to understand more fully the nature of power and what it means to be truly powerful. Specifically, that having power and exercising it is not simply a manifestation of the ego. It need not be "power tripping." It is how I wield my power that matters—making the all-important distinction between creating a situation of power over or power *with*—empowering and having and creating strength in oneself and others. Being powerful is a big responsibility.

To put all this another way: Do I choose to create situations in which I am able to wield power over others? Or do I choose to empower others, sharing my strengths with them, while nurturing their strengths as well? The first is not true power. It is control. The second, I believe to be the essence of true and positive power: strength. It is integral to creating a more harmonious world.

While this may be apparent, even basic to others, it was an *aha!* moment for me. Too often in the years ahead I would give away my power and question my own strength. Time and again, however, my inner strength, my shadow teacher's gift, helped me survive and thrive until I could take responsibility for and embrace more fully my own power.

6.
EFFORT VS. SURRENDER

"Every living being is an engine geared to the wheelwork of the universe. Though seemingly affected only by its immediate surrounding, the sphere of external influence extends to infinite distance."
~ *Nikola Tesla*

I had just come in from my usual run through Burlington's tony Hill Section, a beautiful residential area overlooking Lake Champlain. It was late summer, in 1978, and the smell of autumn was just beginning to tinge the late afternoon air. It had been a good run.

My phone was ringing. (Remember this was way before cell phones, and I had no answering machine back then and so no caller ID—no reason to.) I reached for the phone where it hung on the dining-room wall.

"Hello?"

"Hello, may ah speak tah whoevah is in chahge of sales, please?" a thickly southern accent on the other end of my phone inquired. I almost said "Huh?!" out loud before remembering our ad had just broken in *Running Times* magazine and it had my home phone as Jogbra's contact number.

"Uh, I can help you," I said, hoping that was true.

"Well, missy, mah name is Jimmy Pickens, and I'm a sales rep with a firm down heah in Atlanta, Georgia. We cover the southeast down heah—call on all the finest sporting goods stores—and we were wonderin' if y'all were looking foah reps, and if so p'haps we could help each othah out."

I had no idea. I hadn't understood much of what he'd said after he gave me his name, and my confusion had nothing to do with his accent. "Well, Mr. Pickens, I don't know. I don't know . . . uh, what's a rep?"

There was a very long pause on the other end of the line, and then this sweet gentleman drew in his breath and asked me, very politely, if we might happen to be new to the sporting goods business, to which I replied, "Uh, yes, um . . . yes, we are."

"Well, if y'all have a moment, I'll 'splain how this works . . ."

For the next hour and twenty minutes, Mr. Pickens generously, kindly gave me a thorough tutorial on how the sporting goods business actually worked. There in my dining room/office, I slid down the wall and sat on the floor, kicked off my running shoes, and—with the phone cradled against my ear—took copious notes. He explained how commissions worked and the difference between shoe, apparel, and accessory commissions. He suggested trade shows we should consider attending and why. I think we even discussed whether the Jogbra was apparel or an accessory.

In effect, Mr. Jimmy Pickens taught me exactly how to get the Jogbra into stores all over the southeast . . . and—it dawned on me during the conversation—the rest of the United States as well, because these "sales representatives" were, he assured me, all over the country.

"I send you samples . . . for *free*?" I remember asking. (It's so embarrassing now to recall my total lack of knowledge.)

Southern gentleman that he was, Mr. Pickens just chuckled. "Yes, ma'am. Thank ya' kindly. It would be helpful to have somethin' to actually show mah customers, don't y'all agree?"

By the end of that phone call, I'd hired Mr. Pickens as our first sales rep! And he and his firm sold a lot of Jogbras in Georgia and the Carolinas; they were with us for years.

This was one of the first in a long line of kindnesses and generous bits of help shown to us. People were so willing to help, to answer our questions, to show us how or why—and sometimes why not.

Starting and running this business was always about learning, gaining information, and then accruing the knowledge to apply it correctly. In yoga, there is a concept of reaching a balance between effort and surrender.

Another discipline refers to it as "reach and withdraw." And knowing when to engage in one versus the other is wisdom. This was, for me, an important and constant lesson to be learned at my business's knee.

In 1978's hot and muggy August, Hinda left South Carolina and drove north. She went to New York City and paid a visit to Polly, and then continued up to Vermont to my house. She burst through my back door and came through the kitchen in a flurry. Since Hinda had only just arrived back in Burlington, I offered her a place to stay. Remember, I was new at this living alone thing, and she needed someplace until she found her own apartment. It was the natural thing to do—what friends did for one another, of course—and for me it killed two birds with one stone: it would make doing the business stuff way easier and I wouldn't be living alone quite yet.

But then things took an odd turn. As best I can remember it, after the hellos and establishing that she could stay with me while apartment hunting, the pithy part of our subsequent conversation went something like this:

"So, you are really moving to Vermont now, Hinda?"

"Oh, I'm here." She gave me what I remember as a rather sidelong look. "The bras are on their way up here, and I am going to do this bra biz. Are you?"

I didn't think I'd heard her right. "What?"

"Look, Lisa, I'm going to do this bra business. Are you? If not, I will buy your shares. Are you with me or not?"

I was surprised, to say the least. Was I with her? I felt complete ownership around my jock bra, now Jogbra. It had never entered my mind not to do this "bra biz," as she called it. This idea that I had created, was busy creating . . . it was my baby! Hadn't I just offered to turn my apartment into our workspace? Wasn't my address in a goddamned magazine ad for the bra? What was she thinking? I started babbling.

"*Buy* my shares? *What? No!* And, yes, of course I'm gonna do Jogbra, Hinda! I can do this and go to grad school—it's perfect. You'll stay here until you're on your feet. We'll turn the living room into a warehouse and office. Polly can be helping on the New York end of things! It'll all work!" I think I was trying to reassure her. Remind her.

At the end of the summer before, the three of us had shared a common vision, sitting on my living-room floor as we spun out our ideas and possibilities for this new bra for women runners. We envisioned a women-for-women enterprise, one where friends worked together in an atmosphere of trust and mutual support, making a good product, and creating our own financial stability and independence in the process. We would be free of the restrictions and prejudices of Corporate America. This was very important to me. Working for myself was a way to create real freedom from the epilepsy-related employment discrimination I'd faced in the past. This Jogbra business could be my ticket to a kind of freedom that few people around me even knew I needed. (In later years, I would learn I was not alone. Unemployment and underemployment are huge issues for people with epilepsy.)

But here I was now, on a sunlit August day almost a year after that important conversation between the three of us, feeling a very different kind of energy. The memory of our earlier conversation and its vision struck me, and I turned and looked her in the eye and said, "We'll work together, Hinda. By women, for women! Together. Remember?"

She merely shrugged. In an abrupt, offhand manner Hinda said, "I bought Polly's shares in Jogbra."

I was stunned.

Hinda talked on. What she was saying so surprised me that I had difficulty processing it.

She told me that when she visited Polly in New York City she had asked Polly the same question about continuing with the Jogbra business, to which, Hinda reported, Polly had replied that, no, she wasn't interested in continuing with Jogbra. So Hinda bought eighty of Polly's one hundred shares.

I couldn't speak. I must be confused. *What did she say?* My heart began to race. *Polly sold most of her shares to Hinda?*

I had known Polly wasn't interested in being part of the daily grind of the business. She had made that clear early on. I accepted that. My understanding of Polly's path—her heart being in her costume design world—was part of why I'd invited Hinda to join us last summer. But Polly had left me with the strong impression that she wanted to continue to be involved somehow. We had a long history of being creative together, bouncing ideas off one another. I was really surprised by this, by Hinda's news about this transaction—and more than a little hurt. I was really disappointed that Polly was so uninterested that she would give up her shares and do so without speaking to me about it first. As Hinda's words continued to sink in, I still didn't quite understand the implications, especially the implications for our roles in the business.

Oh well, I thought, trying to calm myself as all this flashed through my brain. *There's still Hinda.* She was standing there in the middle of my dining room, looking down at me as I sat at my oval wooden table and not saying anything more after dropping her bombshell.

"I'm so sorry to lose Polly!" I said, still in shock. "Oh, well, I'll pay you whatever you paid her for half of those shares, re-equalize. We'll go forward, Hinda—you and me. What did you pay her for them?" I was still trying to process the situation. Babbling, I tried to envision how it would be working with just Hinda and no Polly, my longtime friend. I'd never really considered that before. "Well, whatever! I'll reimburse you, and we will redistribute the shares between us—you and me. We'll figure it—"

"No," Hinda interrupted.

"What?"

"No, Lisa. I'm not selling you any shares. But like I said, I'll buy *your* shares. I'm willing to make you the same offer I gave her."

Surprised, I declined again, this time realizing that Hinda was being quite serious. I looked at her anew then. Climbing out of my shock and upset to focus more acutely on this messenger, on Hinda, I saw something had changed. It was clear she wasn't the same person who had left Vermont the summer before. Last summer, I'd met a woman full of joy, who sparkled and laughed. Now that sparkle was gone and there was a fire in its place, and not a warm one. She was icy. And angry. I wondered why.

Again, I offered to pay her whatever she had paid Polly to equalize our share distribution. Again, she declined, saying that it was her intent to be in charge, to be the boss of Jogbra. *She* was now the majority shareholder, she declared, and I must do as she said or she would fire me. She would fire *me!* I didn't even know if that was possible! Inside I was shaking, but my shock was quickly being riddled with incredulity and anger. What had happened to the yoga-teaching, vegetarian, enthusiastic, women-for-women person I had enlisted into my Jogbra project just one year ago? Why was she now so different? Who was this new woman looking down at me in my own home? Power tripping! Was she threatening me?

The conversation eroded into what would turn out to be the first of many arguments about the issue of ownership in my fledgling business. And I do not deal well with confrontation, especially the kind where voices are raised. And they were raised.

No resolution in sight, we each retreated. Hinda went to collect her bags and boxes of stuff from her car and went on up into my guest room. I went out onto the humid streets of Burlington's summer evening to try to run—literally jog some sense of peace and order into my confused psyche. Back then I tried to tell myself, *Don't worry, she's just having a bad day.*

When I called Polly the next day to find out why she had sold her shares, she told me Hinda had given her the distinct impression that I was no longer interested in pursuing my Jogbra business.

"Hinda said that with you being in school and splitting up with Al and all—that you are not really interested in our Jogbra anymore! That isn't true? And I, well, I certainly wasn't going to stay involved if *you* weren't, Lisa."

"Why didn't you call me, Pol? Ask me?" I'm sure I sounded frantic.

"I didn't think to. Hinda told me . . . I didn't think Hinda would have any reason to, uh, to . . . And she said she was in a rush, only had an hour or two . . . Oh god, Lisa! I'm so sorry!" The implications were beginning to sink in.

I got off the phone with Polly as quickly as I could—I had to process all my conflicting feelings. I felt sick to my stomach. I was angry, dizzy. A first, visceral reaction had been fury toward Polly—fury and incredulity. How could she be so stupid! But right behind that was an immediate quashing of that feeling; I wouldn't allow myself to be angry with Polly—my Polly, my best friend. No! This was not her fault! She'd been trusting, taken the word of a presumed friend.

But then came another wave of fury toward Hinda: How dare she!

As soon as I could get an appointment to see him, I went to the lawyer who had set up the corporation to see if Hinda's maneuver was legal. Unfortunately, he had neglected to advise me to create an agreement that provided a safeguard to prevent one shareholder from buying shares from another without the consent of all the shareholders. In a grave tone, sitting across from me behind his big, polished mahogany desk he said, "It's legal. She has a legal right to buy your other partner's shares. It may be unethical, Lisa, but it's not illegal." It struck me that he didn't apologize for omitting this pertinent—and I discovered later, standard—clause when he'd drawn up our partnership agreement.

Polly and I were confused by what had transpired, by who Hinda had seemed to have become over the past year. But we did not discuss what had happened much more. I think we were both too wounded. And what was there to say? We had both trusted Hinda—Polly had made her decision to sell her shares based on misleading information she had been told by her, and, for my part, I had trusted Hinda enough to include her in the original share distribution even though I barely knew her. Then, as luck would have it, I had hired a lawyer who had clearly not drafted a complete and protective incorporation document. It was a perfect storm.

I was furious. I was indignant. I felt powerless. I had no idea what I could do to undo what had been done. And the confusion I was feeling—along with all those other reactions—was also laced with embarrassment, shame. The summer before, I had made a decision, based on the information and evidence I had, to make Hinda my partner in my bra business start-up. I'd offered her those one hundred shares because of my "by women, for women" mindset. Or so I could tell myself. But really, wasn't my decision in part based on fear? Why did I need partners at all? Because I was afraid to go it alone, and now I was ashamed about the mess I found myself in because of my fears.

So, because I felt responsible for the situation and was unwilling to abandon my new business, I stuffed my feelings of betrayal and hurt into a tight little box, sticking it away in a corner of my being. I was hoping that Hinda was just going through a bad phase and would not continue to uphold this inequity for long. *Yoga woman will be back,* I told myself. My "nice-girl" ethos and training came in handy here, helping to create behaviors and responses that became placeholders for my more authentic feelings.

Hinda settled into my guest room, the one that Polly had occupied the previous summer, until she could find her own apartment. It was odd; it was tense. I was in varying degrees of denial at all times. I kept thinking that any day now the old Hinda would return, the one from the previous summer. She didn't.

Boxes of bras began to arrive, and the orders started coming in—lots of them. My living room became our warehouse, my dining room our office. There we were at that odd seasonal cusp between summer and fall—me, Hinda, and a lot of cardboard cartons of bras—all crammed in together in my once-lovely home on College Street.

And thus, we started our business together in earnest.

We were scrambling, trying to cover all the required bases to fill the orders that were—amazingly—coming in just from our one small ad and through word of mouth. It was immediately clear that this was right product at the right time!

I had to make a choice between continuing my graduate studies or meeting the demands that Jogbra was placing on me, and my graduate advisor wisely said to me, "Lisa, it seems this business you started is taking off and you need to pay attention to it right now. See what happens, see where it goes. You can always come back to school later."

It was the permission I needed. (Little did I know that it would be thirty years before I actually went back to finish!)

So, one day, having made my decision to let one dream go while pursuing another, I was sitting in my dining-room-turned-office after just getting off the phone with a possible vendor. I knew I needed to meet with him and check out his business in order to consider any next steps. That meant I had to go to his place of business, which was just outside Boston—a three-and-a-half-hour car trip, one way. Uh-oh.

I had just gotten my driver's license a few months before and bought a used Volkswagen Bug. I'd only ever driven it around Burlington, as well as the forty-five minutes down to Montpelier a few times. I'd never driven such a long way by myself, or on major highways. I was sitting there thinking about that when my gaze fell outside, through the window and onto the graying remains of the vegetable garden in the large back yard. Al and I had moved into this apartment in 1973 when we'd moved back to Vermont. We'd chosen this space primarily because it was within walking distance of both downtown and the university *and* was on the bus line—so I could be more flexible about looking for work. Its spacious yard was a bonus. I enjoyed it so much that I was happy to mow it for the landlady. This year, I realized as I looked out the window, I'd totally ignored both the veggie garden and lawn. I wondered who was doing the mowing now.

Hinda came downstairs and inquired as to my apparent inactivity. I told her about the need to go to Massachusetts to interview this gentleman and asked if she also felt it was necessary. She agreed and then went on enthusiastically, "That's great! That's just outside Boston, so you can just go on into Boston and do some sales calls on the same trip! It's perfect!"

There was nothing perfect about it from my perspective. I had been summoning my courage to do the long drive to Massachusetts; now Hinda was escalating the adventure, envisioning an extension into Boston! This was upping the risk from my point of view. I was embarrassed to let her know that idea scared the hell out of me. I was a new a driver, too inexperienced, too timid to take on that length of a trip. Boston was a notoriously difficult city to navigate, even for a seasoned driver, let alone a new one, and one without a navigator.

I hemmed. I hawed. My reticence to immediately and enthusiastically sign on to her plan confused, then infuriated her. She was the boss, the majority shareholder after all, she sternly reminded me. I was to do as she said! This tactic was becoming the "new normal" in any of our interactions where I did not agree with her. I found it tiresome and exhausting and was learning to pick my fights. I had to really think here. When at last I mumbled something about not wanting to drive in Boston, admitting to my fear, she said something derisive, turned on her heel, and went out the door.

I don't know why she didn't offer to go with me or just go herself, if she felt strongly about extending the trip with sales calls. Nor do I recall why it had to be me who went. I did go and meet with the gentleman. We did not end up doing business and I did not drive on into Boston to make sales calls. So why recount this incident at all? Because what I do remember about it are the lessons embedded within, my clear realizations as a result of this exchange.

My first realization, as Hinda left the house, was that I needed to address my relationship with my own fearfulness. How best to confront it, to manage it? Share it or hide it?

And second, right on the heels of the first, I couldn't shake Hinda's reaction. It brought home to me how driving a car is so taken for granted and how surprised—and yes, angry—people can be when faced with another person's differences or limitations. I was perceived as weak, inept. Fearful. I might say I was all those things in that particular circumstance. No wonder I had learned to hide my difference. Should I continue to do so?

The larger lesson of that particular encounter with both Hinda and my own fears was that I was growing. As a driver, I may have been inept and weak, but, as a person, I was strong and getting stronger. I *did* make that trip by myself to near-Boston. And while I still needed to look more closely at the source and nature of any fear I was feeling, I did get in the car.

There is an entry in my journal from 1979 that really took me aback when I reread it recently, because of how early it was in the whole arc of Jogbra's rise. It was remarking on how many people had been telling me what a creative, powerful person I was. So successful! How successful Jogbra was! This was in just our first full year of business, yet already articles had been written about the product, about us, and there was never a lack of orders. So, yes, the perception, both publicly and personally, that Jogbra was a success came right away. Right. Away. And the perception was supported by some impressive numbers. We were profitable our first full year in business and had no idea that this was unusual.

We would continue to grow an average of 25 percent per year during the twelve years that Jogbra remained a privately held company. But back then, in 1978, after driving down almost to Boston and back, all that was in the future. As I pulled into my dark driveway, I felt energized and optimistic, even though the business meeting had not borne fruit. As I clambered out of my battered, old VW Bug and into the late night, I was hugging my own private victory to my metaphoric chest, checking off one of life's smaller achievements: a solo road trip. So what if the milestone had arrived for me a decade or so later than it had for my contemporaries?

7.
BREAST FRIENDS?

"Every man's work, whether it be literature or
music or pictures or architecture or anything
else, is always a portrait of himself."
~ Samuel Butler

Within weeks of Hinda's return to Vermont, it became clear that we were going to need money. Working capital. Orders were coming in, the initial inventory was dwindling, and we needed help—we were going to have to pay people to help us. How were we going to manage without an infusion of capital?

Hinda was speaking with her dad, and she reported that he wanted to buy shares in SLS, Inc. As president of the corporation, I would have to create and issue these shares to him. I still believed that Hinda's aggressive "I'm the boss, do as I say!" stance since buying Polly's shares would soften, and at that point was aware of no other way to raise capital. Knowing fully that it would put me even further in a minority position, I agreed to explore this idea. But it was not to be. As a Canadian citizen, Mr. Schreiber could not hold shares in a US corporation, no matter how small.

While searching for ways to secure financing, I had been directed to the Small Business Administration (SBA). Someone had told me they were full of good, free advice— and they were. It was one of the smartest things I did back in those early days. Ray Denault, the guy we talked with at the SBA, sent me all these forms and made me write up a business plan—a three-year business plan! I think I laughed out loud at the thought. But this was the only way to become eligible for a loan guaranteed by the SBA. No bank was going to give a loan to "two girls with a bra" (as one banker had referred to us) without the SBA's guarantee. The SBA's business plan format forced me to think through every aspect of our fledgling business—cost of goods sold, sales, revenue, profits, salaries, and expenses by categories! Honestly, before doing this, I had never thought about some of those items, and others I had only a vague notion of from my Katie Gibbs quickie-accounting course and selling my stained-glass creations at craft fairs around the state.

Hinda left writing the business plan to me. "You're in graduate school now, Lisa. Think of it as another research paper." It daunted us both, but surprisingly I found I was really glad to be going through the process, even though I was just making up stuff. Really, how many bras were we going to sell each month for the next year?! And the year after that? And after that? And how many of each size each month? And what were we going to spend on advertising? On salaries? We had no history, and I had no idea, so I guessed. I tasked Hinda with speaking with Active Manufacturing and guessing about the factory's production costs in the future and how cost of goods sold ("CGS," a term we'd both just learned) might change over the next three years. I dubbed the whole plan "Financial Fairy Tales" and said a large prayer when, a few intense weeks later, we marched my finished "research paper" down to the local bank, hoping to get an SBA-guaranteed loan.

We did.

Well, we did if we could put up some equity of our own. That was the bank's requirement. And neither of us had any of our own money. So here, Hinda's father stepped in. Since he could not be a shareholder, he generously agreed to loan SLS, Inc. $25,000. A family-based loan, it seemed, was considered personal equity. Fun fact: the interest rate on commercially lent money when we started was around 21 percent. We didn't flinch. We didn't know to flinch. It was just the way things were, what one did in order to do business.

Sometimes ignorance isn't bliss. It just keeps things simple. We were able to get the SBA-guaranteed bank loan, our working capital. Neither one of us being drinkers, we celebrated by going to get a Ben & Jerry's ice cream sundae—with extra chocolate sauce.

In life and business, we each bring our cast of "influencers" along with us into our partnerships. Some are more overtly identifiable than others. These influencers are our unofficial life partners. I felt one of these unofficial partners was Hinda's father, Louis Schreiber. Hinda was influenced by him and her desire to please him. At the time, she would refute this observation, though it was apparent to me and others who came to know and work with her in those early Jogbra days. To be honest, I was grateful for his ability to help.

But the dark side of his monetary loan to us was that from then on—in our ongoing disagreement about our equity positions—Hinda would justify her actions by saying, "It's my money!"

And I would retort, "It is my idea! You wouldn't be here if I hadn't invited you to help me!"

And she would just repeat, not quietly, "It is *my* money!"—meaning, of course, it came from her father's loan to SLS, Inc.

Yet, *we*—not just Hinda—were paying Mr. Schreiber back. It was a loan to the company. Every month the company sent him a check, with interest. Oh, and did I mention? We each had to sign personal guarantees for that SBA-guaranteed bank loan. When I did so I laughed to myself, thinking, "If we default, what are they going to come take? My beat-up, old VW? All my clothing?" I had nothing but my wits and the nascent Jogbra business. But I was on the hook for our big, SBA-guaranteed loan from the bank as much as Hinda was.

From my vantage point in the fall of 1978, I had just jumped out of the frying pan of an emotionally difficult marriage into the fire pit of a dysfunctional business partnership. I would be a liar if I didn't admit that I wondered how it was that I deserved such behaviors from my chosen partners. It made me question: What was wrong with me?

And it hurt. Hinda's behavior toward me was upsetting . . . in part because I honestly did not understand what I had done to deserve it. I spent hours in therapy trying to figure it out—how was I responsible for what was, for me, a difficult work situation? What had I done, said? Was I really such an awful person? I remember one early therapist saying, "You've just come through a difficult marriage and divorce—be kind to yourself." But her comment only reminded me of another person, my ex-husband, who also hadn't seemed to find me worthwhile.

Hinda could be a charming person. I want to be clear here. I'd found her so when we first met. It was my impression that she genuinely wanted to be a part of making this world a better place. But life is complicated, and we all have our shadows.

I just find it so fascinating, and truly ironic, that the sports bra—a true gift to girls and women—was to a great degree born out of such a contentious relationship between two women.

It was powerful fuel for my own inner search and growth.

I cared what other people thought of me, of us. Hinda did not. "I don't care if others like me," she declared more than once. Also, more than once, I felt berated for my of-the-times feminine (read "pleaser") traits. Hinda felt strongly, and often voiced, that there was no difference between men and women. None! My inherent youngest-child traits also seemed to annoy her, as she was the eldest of her siblings. But she did appreciate what she called my "Princess Grace" schtick.

This was something that was just ingrained in me. Too many years of private school, dancing school, formal dinners, and the like. Hinda initially noticed and commented on it when we were first going to the bank and the SBA to try and get the loans to start the business.

"What was that in there?" she asked after we left the loan officer's office.

"What?"

"How you were sitting! And talking, I guess? You were so prim and . . . and proper!" I thought about it. I had sat on the other side of the male loan officer's desk on the edge of the chair. My back was straight, my hands folded in my lap, and my legs were not crossed at the knee, but at the ankles. In retrospect, I probably smiled with my mouth closed and my chin tilted slightly downward.

"Oh, I don't know! It's just how I sit in those sorts of meetings!"

"Yeah! Certainly not like you sit in the office! Ha! You were acting like a princess! Princess Grace!" And from then on, whenever there was an important meeting, Hinda might say, "Pull out your Princess Grace!"

In many ways, Hinda and I were actually perfect partners for each other—if one could just erase the personality conflicts. We complemented each other in terms of our strengths and weaknesses. If this was hard to see, let alone acknowledge to one another back in the day, it nonetheless played out and manifested in our business's success.

An idea person, I always have a vision and want to enroll others to jump onboard. I am also curious and want to understand a thing, a situation, a person. I question everything—even apparent solutions. This can be annoying sometimes, or so I have been told. I can then come up with 6 or 406 different ways and plans for how we might move forward—I like a contingency plan! Because my illness is episodic and unpredictable, I have learned over the course of my life to always have a contingency plan. But this can be both a strength and a weakness, as the perfectionist in me might spend too much time deciding on the best way to proceed. Hinda too, had a trait that could be both a strength and a weakness: she just wanted to move a thing forward, was always quick to forge ahead. Often, when I was still putting the finishing touches on my first plan or comparing and questioning plans 1 to 406, she would have already signed off, sent it off, or was kvetching at me to finish up and get her what she needed.

You get the picture. In actuality, we ended up balancing one another out, while often driving one another crazy as well. But success is also a good teacher: we became able, as the years rolled on, to appreciate each other's proclivity, and to joke about it, laugh about it. See? Perfect partners— at least when we could work together.

I, too, was influenced by my father. As I've mentioned, he was a brilliant marketing man; I like to think I inherited some of his talent and that it showed up in how the Jogbra phenomenon evolved. But Daddy did not manage his money well. He made a lot of money, and lost a lot of money, repeatedly. He was always going to "make a million—it's just around the corner." He became tired of making those millions for the companies who employed him, and at age sixty-four, just shy of corporate retirement, he quit and started his own business to make his own millions—so he said. He bet the farm but had a stroke before that bet could come to fruition, leaving my mother in "difficulties" (as that generation would put it). My siblings and I supported them until their respective deaths.

And it was not lost on me that my father's pattern of great financial successes and losses was not just his. What little I knew of his father, my grandfather, revealed the same pattern. My eldest brother, too, went from wunderkind with a big reputation and paycheck to jobless and homeless in a few short years. This happened more than once. I never knew whether to believe the story of my big brother having to live out of his Porsche at one point in his roller-coaster career.

Observing this familial cycle affected me deeply: I was going to be sure that I avoided that roller coaster and its attendant anxiety. I wanted to be sure to gain a degree of financial stability for myself. And while I'd never started Jogbra as a get-rich-quick scheme, I'm sure this influence saw me through my more difficult times there.

By the time I was starting Jogbra, my father had had that debilitating stroke. He died in 1979, shortly before his seventy-sixth birthday, just as Jogbra was taking off. Daddy never knew his youngest daughter—the one with epilepsy, no less—was the one who actually did "make a million."

By the time May of 1979 had come around, I had completed the required number of credits for my BS in education and gone on and passed the GRE exam. I had even

started taking some of the required courses for my graduate program. No one was more surprised than I was about
my progress. Finally completing my BS, it had been huge
to then be encouraged to go on to graduate school to get
my M.Ed. I was exceeding my own aspirations and loving
every energizing, challenging minute of it. Although it was
an important achievement, something I'd worked toward
for many years, I skipped "walking" at UVM's undergrad
graduation ceremonies in order to fly down and check out
our South Carolina sewing facility. What the heck, I told
myself, no one was going to go with me to watch me walk.
I was, remember, an "older" student, married but separated,
with ill and elderly parents who lived in another state.
Nope, this event was not on any family calendar.

So, on that particular graduation day, I was not in a
cap and gown; I was in an airplane heading to a place I
had never been before—both literally and metaphorically.
I was going to meet JD and Caroline and see how they
were producing our bra for jogging. Hinda and I took our
consultant-really-tutor Dick Kohler with us—I think to
help JD and Caroline (as much as us) get in our manufacturing groove. I recall sitting on the airplane on the way
down and noticing all these men in their business suits.
I was struck that they were all reading newspapers, paying no attention to the view outside the airplane window
or, seemingly, to the flight itself. Me, I was so excited! I

remember thinking, "I'll never be so jaded as to take air travel for granted like that!" Ha! Silly me . . . little did I know.

I'd never been to Columbia before and was impressed with the city. I saw it by going for a run there, with Hinda. I remember this run, as it was one of the few times that Hinda and I went on a run together. Around that time, I was running about thirty miles a week, averaging around six miles a day—back then often difficult to do in an unknown place, especially for a woman on her own. And I preferred to run alone, and when I did run with others it would be with those who did the same sort of distance. Hinda had only recently started jogging, in part, I think, because of our business. Her lifelong passion was downhill skiing, something she had done since childhood.

But on this day, it was curiosity and sightseeing that took predominance over going any distance. And what a city! I found it beautiful. I have no idea where exactly we were in the city, but I remember lots of greenery and trailing vines with colorful blossoms on them—rare treats to my Vermont-ish eyes.

What does it say about me that I recall little about the visit to the factory itself? I think that because I saw that the factory was clean and I found JD and Caroline were sincere, honest, hardworking people, I felt good about everything. And because my business partner was thoroughly enmeshed in this end of the business, I trusted all was being handled. For these reasons and more, I simply didn't feel the need to remember it. But I do remember the excitement and joy of that run, of that time, and of my overall positive feeling about a universe of possibilities spinning out in front of us.

8.
THE GROWING GODDESSES

"The simplest and most basic meaning of the symbol of the Goddess is the acknowledgment of the legitimacy of female power as a beneficent and independent power."
~ *Carol P. Christ*

The US Small Business Administration (SBA) existed in every state and had lending quotas to fill—it had to lend a certain amount of its funds to minorities. In the 1970s, women were considered a minority in the business community. Between our gender, my business plan, some family financing, and a small local bank, a loan to manufacture and sell a bra was granted to two women with little to no business experience. Miracles do happen!

Except it was no miracle. It took vision, hard work, courage, and perseverance.

It is my experience that one cannot successfully grow an idea into a reality that manifests as a real-world business without also growing as much, or more, personally. By its very nature, growth is change. In order to both anticipate and respond to my growing enterprise, I too had to grow and change. I had to confront, challenge, and work at my own stuff, my own baggage—an opportunity handed to me almost daily because my business partner and I had such differing values and operating styles.

These days, the issue of women and power is a socio-political hot topic. In my business partnership and the primarily male industry in which the Jogbra business operated, I came to think quite a bit about the subject of power and my own perceptions of power or lack of it. What role did character play? Inner strength? Was being a strong person the same as being a powerful person?

Power doesn't have a gender. Strength is an acquired trait that is honed by adversity and challenge. Living with and through our vulnerabilities is a vital part of the process if we are to successfully transform and grow.

How do we think about women and power and ambition, really? Remember, I embarked on the Jogbra enterprise in the late '70s and built it throughout the '80s. An ambitious woman desiring to become or remain successful, a person with a degree of power, was parroting the male model. At the time, there was no alternative to that narrative. We wore business suits with shoulder pads. Being "assertive" was touted and taught, but too many of us mixed that up with being "aggressive," which was so easily viewed and learned in our male-dominated culture. And either characteristic could backfire in the all-male board-room. Yet, in routine business settings, I might also witness many smart, opinionated, and strong-willed women become flirty, coy, and flattering toward their male counterparts as a matter of course in order to move the business agenda forward. Both my business partner and I were among them, playing the role. Bring on "Princess Grace"! It was the norm, in the then and there.

Yet, while we female baby boomers were raised to be wives, secretaries, nurses, and teachers, the so called "sexual revolution" was beginning to change all that. We became the first generation of young women who believed we could "have it all"—families and any career we chose. We could "bring home the bacon and fry it up in a pan," as the iconic Enjoli™ perfume commercial touted. Day care blossomed. And after putting in the hours and years of juggling education, career, and family, what happened? The boomer generation of power-suited working women nonetheless encountered the corporate "glass ceiling." To be The Boss was unusual, an anomaly, unless you were an entrepreneur and it was your own business.

But things were evolving, nonetheless, sometimes in ways more subtle than the flash of celebrity exposés or righteousness of indignant political marches and speeches. In kitchens, offices, and classrooms, the inexorable and indefatigable modern women's psyche was morphing. Living with and through our vulnerabilities proved a vital part of the process in our successful transformations. Mine included.

At Jogbra, it was the power of our belief in the need for the product, our strength to persevere through the unknown, our ability to learn on our feet, and our passion that drove us forward. We were dedicated to our mission because we knew that the sports bra removed a real barrier for women and girls in their quest to reach, to stretch, to grow and become stronger.

These days, we talk as a nation about all different sorts of power—political, corporate, national, global, male, female—and all the variant abuses thereof. A person's insecurity and fear can foster the need to create "power over" another, the all-too-familiar power struggle motif of our current dominator culture. We like to think this is a very male model, but it was a facet in our very female Jogbra culture. And it pained me. I could see it, feel it, and—begrudgingly—I engaged in it. I had not quite figured out how to do this dance differently. Oh, we had some yoga classes in the warehouse early on. We did New Age trainings for our managers, and later a "360" that involved all the staff. While these were helpful to some degree, they all felt a bit like window dressing—a business version of the "now-I'm-supposed-to" of the gravy '80s. In large part this was because I never had the trust or friendship of my partner—a basic ingredient in any authentic leadership team that seeks to empower others.

But that did not, could not, stop what was occurring in my personal world. What is the old saying, "What doesn't kill you will make you stronger"? I was not going to let the crap, the ways in which I was weak and vulnerable, kill me. I would not—would try my very best to not—let people wield power over me. Instead, I was going to get stronger, to draw upon and nourish my inner strength. I was already becoming stronger . . . so much stronger. I was becoming more independent, confronting my epilepsy-infused fears (both real and imagined), and figuring out how to grow and learn to be in a productive relationship with someone who saw me as an adversary.

9.
MARKETING 101

"The two words 'information' and 'communication' are often used interchangeably, but they signify quite different things. Information is giving out; communication is getting through."
~ *Sydney J. Harris*

Once we figured out *where* to sell the Jogbra, it was time to figure out *how* to reach our customers. After hiring our bookkeeper, packing and shipping person, and an administrative assistant, I knew we needed an ad agency. Enter Sandage Advertising and Marketing—run, of course, by a powerful, opinionated woman. Great! Just what we needed: another one in the mix!

Barbara Sandage was a standout in those days. Funny, smart, ambitious, and more than a decade older than me. She was truly a mold breaker. She would never refer to herself as a feminist, but her actions branded her as one. It was clear she had learned "the old ways" that women used to get by: she flattered, flirted, cajoled, smiled. But being widowed (her first husband was killed in Vietnam), divorced, very smart, a survivor, and the mother of two girls and one son, Barbara had learned to channel her strengths. She found the allies she needed, courted and kept helpful friends, advised and nursed wounded friends, and played a mean game of poker—for serious money.

Barbara was an excellent businesswoman—no small thing in the cutthroat advertising and marketing world. With her undergraduate degree in psychology and an MFA from Yale, she was well equipped for the advertising game. Barbara knew her stuff. She was generous with her knowledge, teaching me a great deal during the many years we worked together. And we had fun. She made me laugh. Happily, she gained as well from her years with Jogbra. Her firm grew with us, right up to the day we sold our company.

A natural division of responsibilities between Hinda and I occurred. While Hinda focused on learning the production side of the business, going back and forth to South Carolina—and in later years to Puerto Rico and the Far East—I was on College Street in Vermont wrangling with Barbara about positioning, marketing messages, packaging, and collateral materials or on the road interviewing, hiring, and working with our sales representatives and their sporting goods accounts. Yes, Hinda and I both were involved in all aspects of our business—we had to be. But we each had areas to which we naturally gravitated and excelled. In that respect, we were perfect partners.

Like the product itself, our sizing and our packaging were revolutionary. They had to be. Bras in sporting goods stores? Unheard of. For both point-of-sale as well as production and cost concerns, the original Jogbra sizes were limited to small, medium, and large. Sporting goods stores could only handle this limited number of stock-keeping units (SKUs). There were other accommodations that needed to be made and questions to be addressed. For one, how do you display a bra in a sporting goods store? It had never been done before. Barbara and her team came up with the perfect solution: folded bras in see-through plastic bags with a straightforward, explanatory cardboard insert—brilliant!

A fun aside: one of Sandage's early account execs working on Jogbra was Chris Bohjalian, who is now a well-known and prolific author (*Midwives*, *The Sandcastle Girls*, *The Flight Attendant*). His books have even been made into movies. Back then, though, he authored some fun and very effective promotions and ad copy. One scheme in particular, which I believe was his brainstorm, took place in the mid-1980s after we had experienced some very real acceptance and success. We were having an ongoing conversation about stimulating our "Public Relations"—which really meant trying to stretch our advertising and marketing budget by dreaming up ways to get press and our customers' attention without having to pay for it—when Chris came up with a great idea.

Not long before this brainstorming session, we'd sent one of our early original Jogbras to the Metropolitan Museum of Art in New York City and they had seen fit to put it in their costume collection, labeled as "a revolutionary piece of women's undergarments, circa 1977." We thought this was wonderful (I still do!) and sent out lots of press releases about our Jogbra's inclusion in such a prestigious collection. So, there we were in Sandage's conference room brainstorming about how we might replicate such a feat—wondering who else we might send an original, early Jogbra to and then tell everyone about it.

"Well, there is one problem with that idea," I said. "We don't have any more original bras. We sold them all." I think I laughed, rather delighted with that now inconvenient fact.

Hinda was at that meeting and she confirmed my statement. "Yeah, I think the one that went to the Metropolitan is one I found in the back of my closet. I don't know of any others."

And this is where the imagination that fuels Chris Bohjalian's novels today popped up all those years ago in service of the Jogbra. "Let's ask for some back," he proposed. "For some of those old bras back . . . from our customers. If you had an old one in your closet, Hinda, I bet some other women do, too. They are so well made, they last forever! We could do a PR campaign where we offer our customers a new Jogbra for *free* if they have an old, original style #101 and send it back to us! Maybe one of them will even be in good enough shape to donate to another museum! It will be our next PR push!"

Well, this was just brilliant, and unheard of at the time in the sporting goods industry, not to mention we were talking about women's underwear! It was effective, too. We didn't really get that many bras back—not of the correct style, anyway. But we did get a fair amount of free ink for not a lot of investment on our part. And it was fun, and funny!

But that incident happened years later. At this stage we were just honing our skills, gearing up to present ourselves to the industry at the NSGA (National Sporting Goods Association) trade show in Chicago in February of '79. It would be our "coming out" party. The goal was to officially debut our product there and hire more sales reps. In the meantime, we were doing what we could—getting the packaging and collateral material ready (the term I'd learned that meant sell sheet, order form, and such). Mostly, we were just looking to get more Jogbras in more stores. So, off we went on the road to sell our bras. As 1978 was rolling into its last quarter, Hinda was following up in North and South Carolina and I went off to California. The resistance I encountered when I went selling on the road was, in retrospect, pretty funny.

It was common knowledge—really that era's version of an urban myth—that all athletic and health trends got their start in California. So, off I went. I packed my running shoes and brand new big-lady-business suit-cum-shoulder-pads and picked up my Samsonite briefcase that was holding a dozen packaged bras, our new sell sheets and, most importantly, order forms. I also had a map of San Francisco, as I'd never been there before.

I landed at the San Francisco Airport the day after Thanksgiving. The plan was that I would stay at a friend of a friend's place in the city. This was before we had any significant money budgeted for travel (I had made the expense number up, remember, in my "Financial Fairy Tales" plan for the bank) and we were operating on the proverbial shoestring. The friend of a friend was named Pat, and she welcomed me warmly into her home. After showing me to my room, she introduced me to her friend, Val, who had just stopped in.

"Val's husband is coming by later and we're all going to do Thanksgiving leftovers for dinner. Join us!" Pat said. "You must be tired and hungry after your trip!" I replied that I'd love to, and she left me to my unpacking.

There I stood, in that unfamiliar house, in a strange and beautiful city, wondering what to do next. I had no idea how I was going to do what I was supposed to do. I had just recently, finally, passed my driver's license test back in Vermont. I did not have much driving experience, and I had never rented a car, and so I was not about to do so in a busy and unfamiliar city, full of traffic—I wasn't going to drive around looking for unknown addresses. (Yup, again, no Google Maps.) Most of my life, I had gotten around by taking buses. As a teenager living in New York City, I preferred the buses to the subway. Of course, I didn't know the bus system in San Francisco, so I was going to have to do some research. But that's how I decided to tackle the problem of making cold sales calls in San Francisco.

I located Pat's phone book (remember those?) and the Yellow Pages within (and those?) and looked up "sporting goods stores." I spread open the big paper map of the city and, in the hours before dinner, I compared addresses in the phone book with my street map. I tried to locate as many clusters of sporting goods stores as possible, especially the ones that appeared to be on or near a bus route.

Engaged in plotting my route at Pat's large dining-room table, I became aware of a ruckus just outside the front door: shouting and whooping combined with a clattering noise. Val came from the kitchen where she and Pat had been chatting and opened the large front door. I could see a man in a striped shirt coming up the steep cement stairway, his arms flailing, rather out of control. When he hit the top stair landing in front of the door, I saw why: he was on roller skates! He grabbed Val, skated her backward into the living room, and pushed her down over the back of Pat's chintz-covered couch—his and her legs waving wildly in the air, his wheels still spinning—a surreal and funny tableau. I might have been concerned had the two of them not been laughing uncontrollably.

I sat there awkwardly and quite still, unsure what to make of this strange scene being played out in front of me. Shortly thereafter, I was introduced to Val's rambunctious "attacker." His name was Robin. *Robin Williams*. Pat asked if I had heard of Robin. "He's doing a TV show now. He plays a guy named Mork. And if you haven't figured it out, he's Val's husband," she laughed. So that night, Robin Williams (aka Mork) presided over the recarving of the Thanksgiving turkey, playing mad surgeon on the poor, unsuspecting fowl. Oh, how we all laughed and laughed that evening. It was just what I needed.

The next day, map and notes in hand, I went down to the closest bus stop and examined the transit map posted there. Armed with my list of addresses and paper map of San Francisco, I boarded a bus with my Samsonite briefcase packed with bras. I would pull the cord to stop as I saw the targeted sporting goods store go by. Then, I'd get off the bus and walk back to the store. I would go into each strange domain and ask to speak with whoever did the buying. Sometimes that person was there, sometimes not.

When I got to talk with someone, the conversations usually went something like this:

"What are you selling?"

"The Jogbra! The bra for runners!"

"Ha! We don't (insert 'can't' or 'won't') sell bras here. This is a sporting goods store!"

"Well, you sell jockstraps, don't you?" I'd say, vaguely waving toward the wall where, inevitably, packaged jockstraps hung. This sometimes got their attention, but the one question almost always followed . . .

"I can't carry all those sizes that bras come in."

And it was always such a pleasure to be able to reply, "No problem. We have only three sizes: small, medium, and large. Minimal SKUs for you to manage." I would then pull out our store-friendly plastic bag and show them how it hung nicely on any wall. Just like the jockstraps. And they didn't even have to touch a bra.

Years later, at our tenth anniversary party in 1988 at the NSGA trade show in Atlanta, we gave a "Pioneer Dealer Award" to those first dealers who, in 1978, had been brave enough, visionary enough, to carry a bra in their sporting goods store, and who, ten years later, were still selling them. I had met a few of them for the first time on that maiden trip to San Francisco.

On that first San Francisco sales trip, when I asked Pat about a good running route from her house, she knew just what I meant and where to direct me. In 1978, San

Francisco was big into the jogging craze. But it was also full of steep hills. "Do you like running hills?" she asked. When I laughed and said, "Not like these!" she sat down and sketched out a map that directed me toward the marina and the beach. The beach! Oh, to my beach-girl soul so long trapped in Vermont this was going to be a truly fabulous treat!

Decked out in Jogbra, T-shirt, jacket, shorts, ear cover, and shoes, I went out the door into the crisp air of a San Francisco November day. Off I went. I didn't even care if I got lost. I had a quarter in my pocket with Pat's telephone number written on her sketched map—my idea of emergency preparedness.

I know now that the beach I ran on that day was the one that runs along Highway 1, along the Pacific, down below the famous Cliff House and Seal Rocks. I didn't know that then. All I knew was that I headed west, hit a big street with lots of traffic, crossed it, and had a beach to run on.

Thump, thump, thump went my shoes on the hard-packed sand at the edge of the water. It was flat there, smaller waves frothed and swirled between giant black rocks that shone and jutted up and out, sentinels of the shoreline. The big waves were farther out. I was totally enchanted. This was why I loved running! The beauty of the natural world and I were one, a single, singing, harmonious whole. I felt a part of the wild, gorgeous day and world.

And I was alone. On this foggy November day, no one else was on the beach. As far as my eye could see, there was not another human being in sight. Yet suddenly I felt another presence. I glanced behind me—no one, nothing. I looked up the beach—no one, nothing. I was running north, with the ocean on my left, about a yard from its edge. I glanced over at the water. There, just beneath the swirled surface, I saw a seal following along with me. I was surprised and delighted. I laughed out loud. I didn't stop, though, as this beautiful creature was keeping pace with me, paralleling along through the water. It rolled an eye at me, shot out a little farther into the surf and then back to continue along beside me. It kept up this pattern for the rest of my run along the beach . . . alongside, out, back in, alongside, out, back in . . .

And me, thump, thump, thumping, breathing, smiling, and just totally happy.

It was one of the most magical runs I've ever had.

10.
MARKETING 202

"Everything is alive; everything is interconnected."
~ Cicero

There is an idea that has popped up everywhere from chaos theory to science fiction and New Age memes that is popularly known as the "butterfly effect." Simply put, it is the notion that one very small thing—the movement of a butterfly's wing or the ripple in a lake caused by a pebble being thrown into it—can cause tremendous effect far away: the butterfly's wing a tornado, the ripple a large wave on a distant shore. Cause and effect—does it have limits? The field of physics is telling us that it takes only observation to bring a thing into being. We cannot consider these areas of investigation and not acknowledge that everything—yes, *everything*—is in relationship in some way or another with everything else.

So, it is evident to me that commerce of any kind is also just about relationships. It all boils down, on every level, to this simple concept. While we usually think of relationships as occurring between people, it is far more than that.

I used to teach a course in entrepreneurship specifically for women in The Women's Small Business Program at Trinity College in Burlington, Vermont. I made this concept of relationship and its importance central to how I taught the marketing thought process. I would stress that for a product or service to be successful, it had to meet a perceived need. There is a need, and it wants to be met. Or it may be thought of as a problem to be solved. Or there may be an existing solution that is less than adequate.

For example, in my universe as a runner, there already were a plethora of bras available, but they were inadequate for my purpose. The relationship between my breasts, my running body, and my bra was creating discomfort and distraction. A new solution had to be found, and the relationship occurring when all these things came together had to be fixed. Utilizing this point of view, one sees a set of issues that need to be addressed—they are in relationship with each other and their environment in a way that needs to be changed, adjusted.

Nowhere is this viewpoint truer than in business, as we enter into more and more relationships with people to address all the needs of the organization. Whether designing a product or a service or communicating with others about it—we are in relationship. And meanwhile, how about maintaining a healthy relationship with ourselves?

All the issues we know about stress in the workplace can boil down to an internal balancing act around our relationships: to the work itself, to those we work with, to homelife, to friends and lovers. So quickly those ripples can become waves.

Because Jogbra was growing so quickly, relationships were being discovered, created, ending, expanding, and changing at a pace that makes my head spin to recall—and truly challenged my spirit.

11.
MOVING ON:
24 CLARKE STREET

*"You cannot swim for new horizons until you
have courage to lose sight of the shore."*
~ William Faulkner

I t wasn't long before Hinda found her own apartment in downtown Burlington. We were still operating out of my apartment, and I was still trying to figure out life as a single person. And it seems my landlady at College Street wasn't liking it.

Years later, I would hear crazy tales about the Jogbra start-up in Burlington. Some even made it into print and postings online, and all were really wild. One in particular, about my College Street apartment, was told to me by someone who clearly didn't realize it was my apartment he was talking about. This stranger told me, with great authority, how "they had to cover all the windows with black fabric—or maybe it was paper—to keep what they were doing a secret!"

I think I laughed out loud at the poor guy.

But, no, it wasn't that or other shenanigans, real or imaginary, that made my landlady become disenchanted with me and made me realize that Jogbra-the-business needed to move out of my home. Between the need to hire some help, frequent UPS truck deliveries, and another truck sometimes parked in our driveway—this one a pickup truck driven by a man I had begun seeing—my landlady, Gladys, felt there was too much activity around her home.

It seems I had misjudged Gladys. Far older than I, she was a poet and her husband a well-known Vermont artist with a gallery up at the university named after him. I considered them fellow artists, albeit from the "Beat Generation," and fancied them kindred spirits. I had confided in Gladys on occasion, sitting cross-legged in her little study in the "big house," just a wall away from where my dining room was now the Jogbra offices. Well, there I went, assuming again—always dangerous. Because Gladys was not tolerant of my newly separated status. She was more a woman of her times than the avant-garde, freethinking poet I had thought her to be. She had been comfortable with me in her house as the wife of Al, the former seminarian, churchgoer, and social worker. Knowing nothing of our personal life on the other side of her walls, it seemed to her I must be at fault in the failure of the marriage. She let me know that she did not approve of my new status and especially "my friend" and his pickup truck in her driveway. I think she even sniffed when she said it. She was generous, however, saying I might take as long as I needed to find another place. But the message was clear: both Jogbra and Lisa had to find new homes. For me, it was emotionally daunting—losing my husband, my married life, and now my beloved home and garden, a place that had in great part contributed to my newfound courage to move toward autonomy.

But really, it made sense. Needing help, we had hired Kate as our "administrative assistant" as soon as we knew the SBA loan was going through. She was another quick brain, another pair of hands. And I was down at the accountant's office interviewing bookkeepers—where were we going to put that person when hired?

Luckily, it wasn't difficult finding office space in Burlington back then. Before the snow started falling (an important consideration when contemplating moving in Vermont) we were in 24 Clarke Street. We transformed what had been a doctor's office into Jogbra's new offices. Boy, did we feel official! It was the first floor of an old house—once someone's home—in Burlington's downtown area, just a block away from Church Street. From Clarke Street we could walk to get lunch, or just out and away. UPS could get to us, and there was a bit of parking in the driveway.

The building itself was what I thought of as a "quasi-Victorian," with a gabled roof, big front porch, and shingles—but it wasn't grand at all. If it had ever had lawns or grounds of any measure, they had long since been sold off to build more housing, with only room for driveways between them.

We installed Kate in the front room, the old "reception" area. Hinda and I each had our own office. Mine was in what I thought had once been the living room/waiting room. It had three large windows, in front of which I put the big, old oak desk from my apartment. This desk had been custom built for my grandfather when he was superintendent of the Brooklyn school system, or so I was told. And my mother had memories of hiding in its kneehole as a little girl.

Across from my desk was a boarded-up fireplace. Above its mantel I hung a huge, plastic-covered—so I could write on it—map of the United States. On it I would draw lines around each rep group's territory as I hired them. I needed something visual to keep track of the reps and the geography. I mean, really, I couldn't recall off the top of my head that Nebraska was east of Wyoming, or where Kentucky was in relation to Tennessee. With this map I was able to figure out who worked next to whom and how it might make sense to line up piggyback visits out in the field.

One of the other rooms had been the doctor's X-ray room, complete with lead-lined walls and no windows—and yes, we used it as an office. Our newly hired bookkeeper was the lucky occupant. We combined an enclosed back porch with the kitchen area to create some warehouse space and an area for packaging and shipping.

We were in a hiring frenzy. Along with Kate and our new bookkeeper, we needed to hire someone for the packing and shipping duties. I remember that this felt like a big step. Up until that point, we had been doing it ourselves on an as-needed basis, with the occasional help of friends. We even used to go out and scout dumpsters looking for cardboard boxes suitable for use to ship our bras! It was a big leap from that to hiring someone. To need someone forty hours a week just to receive the inventory from the factory, inspect it, put it in packages, and then ship it out to customers! Why, we even started buying our very own cardboard shipping boxes! That made me feel—*know*—that we were officially in business. One of the very first people we hired as our packing and shipping clerk, Lydia, stayed with us for years, moved into management, and, I heard, eventually came to run her own business.

It is another by-product of Jogbra, another outcome— the lives that were touched. So many people, mostly women, who may have started with us back then and became entrepreneurs themselves or are now upper management in corporate America. It makes me feel that the idea of the jock bra did far more than just support women in athletics—it supported and continues to support women to be strong in themselves. Period. I love that.

But back then, in those very early days, periodically Hinda and I would still do "pizza nights." This was when the perfect storm of a big and long-awaited shipment of product from the factory would arrive at the same time that we had lots of orders waiting to be shipped out to our retail customers. At these times, we all had to pitch in and do receiving, quality control, and packaging duty.

Everyone would stay late, and we would form an assembly line. The first person in the line would unpack the bras that had been sent in bulk from the factory in South Carolina. We had to make sure that we got what we were supposed to get and were being charged for ("receiving"). Then someone would look at each bra to make sure it was up to our standards (quality control) while keeping them sorted by size. The next person would fold each bra carefully, so that the next person in our little assembly line could insert the folded bra in its plastic-bag packaging with its cardboard insert, again keeping all the sizes and, eventually, colors organized. This process would create our inventory for "fulfillment"—meaning the next day we could fill the stack of orders sitting in the front office, because now our inventory was checked in and ready to be shipped out to our retail customers. Hey, when you are an entrepreneur you not only order and pay for the pizza, you stay and wash the dishes, too!

While in our Clarke Street offices, we grew tremendously. We went from creating the basics—order forms, packaging, and organizational systems (although we didn't know to call them that then)—to a full-time staff of eight. We'd put on retainer an advertising and marketing firm, an accounting firm, lawyers, as well as a business consultant and were utilizing them all regularly as we dealt with the ever-increasing production, financial complexities, and legal questions that arose in our fast-growing business. I used to refer to our consultant, Dick Kohler, as my private tutor! Thank God for him!

Back in the fall of 1977, when I was going back and forth with my brother-in-law about how to bring my idea and its prototype to market, I instinctively knew I needed some sort of patent protection; it was just a matter of finding out who, where, how. I quickly learned that there were no patent attorneys in Burlington, Vermont. Yet, once again, serendipity stepped in.

Shortly after we had moved into our "new" offices at 24 Clarke Street in Burlington, I found myself in a long line at the large post office downtown. My task that day was probably buying stamps or mailing invoices. Remember, in those early days we were doing everything: packaging bras, stuffing shipments, labeling—everything but the bookkeeping and office cleaning. Those last two I knew to hire others to do. (The first to keep track of our finances better than I would or could, the second because I just didn't want to end my workday dusting and vacuuming. Truth.)

So, standing there in line, a conversation started up between myself and the guy in front of me. He told me he was an entrepreneur himself and when he learned what my business was, like so many he was intrigued and started asking questions. I was only too happy to blather on. And it came up that I was in the process of trying to get my product patented. He bemoaned with me the dearth of any help in the area and said, "You gotta go straight to DC. Don't mess around. That's where the patent office is, that's where the good patent attorneys are. If you are interested, I've got a great guy!"

And that's how I found the firm to do our patent work. This post office guy wrote down the name—Roger Browdy, Browdy & Neimark—and a phone number on a scrap of paper and handed it to me. I walked back to our office, picked up the phone, and called them.

It is a long procedure to get a patent. And quite a learning process. To begin with, there are different kinds of patents—like design and utility—then searches for pre-existing "art" must be done, drawings and specifications of your product must be submitted, and the paperwork is voluminous. In 1978 there were no computers and no internet, so this was a time-consuming process with lots of photocopying, faxes, phone calls, and endless back-and-forthing.

One awkward moment was when Browdy & Neimark called for our official drawings of the original product for the submission and I realized none really existed outside of the rough sketches Polly or I had casually drawn on various scraps of paper back in my apartment—a time that now seemed oh-so-long ago. Well, Hinda was trained as a costume designer as well, so I turned to her to create the necessary "official" drawings.

But Hinda chose not to do the drawings and told me to ask Polly to draw up some official sketches. Since Polly was listed on the patent application, I could see the logic in this, so I gave her a call. After all, I was listing all three of us on the patent application: Eugenie Zobian Lindahl ("Lisa" is my nickname, and I wanted this to be very official and legal-schmegal!), Polly Palmer Smith, and Hinda S. Schreiber. Frankly, I secretly felt naming Hinda on the patent was being gracious on my part if one took literally the definition of a patent as claiming ownership of an idea and conception of the product. But I was grateful for Hinda's great ability to move things forward, and including her acknowledged that she had been the one to actually get the damn thing into a factory and manufactured—what in patent terms is "reducing the invention to practice," and is no small task.

So as that autumn progressed, so did the patent process. I was shepherding it along with all the other items on my list (and it was a long list). Get order forms made. Do a sell sheet. Take photos for sell sheet. Ads? Put ads in paper for shipping clerk. Research trade shows. Call all reps. Sales? How to keep track of everything? Filing systems? Forward Polly's sketches to Browdy & Neimark. Go over bookkeeping with Ruth. Did I mention I was negotiating my divorce from Al amid all this chaos? I needed a break.

An incredible opportunity came my way as the year was drawing to an end. A friend of mine had moved to Sri Lanka and invited me to come visit her there. Sri Lanka! Ancient Ceylon, island of tea, rubies, and Eastern mysteries! Wow! I so wanted to go. Travel had always been high on my list, such a rich form of learning experience for me. I started puzzling out how to have this adventure and handle my work obligations as well.

Traveling halfway around the world meant this could not be a quick trip; I needed two weeks at least. I figured that with Christmas and New Year's coming up business would be slow anyway, and what the heck—I didn't have a family to have holidays with anymore. I looked at my list of tasks and realized there were those things I could do ahead of time, those that could be put off without consequences, and a couple that, yes, someone would need to watch and respond to while I was gone. One of those was the patent process and the communications with the patent attorneys.

When I laid out my plan, Hinda agreed to my two-week absence and said she would take on those tasks that needed attention while I was gone. Reason number one for having a partner!

I was very excited about this trip. I had never been anywhere as exotic as Sri Lanka, never in a culture so different from the Western world in which I was brought up. I spent Christmas Eve in an airplane—two Christmas Eves, actually, because we crossed the international date line. The plane was full of Germans, and we sang lots of Christmas carols, sometimes in English! And I had a sumptuous Christmas dinner the next day at the rather lavish home of an attaché to the US Embassy in Colombo. The following two weeks flew by, and Jogbra was a world away. Suffice to say here that I quickly learned that one of the perks of being an entrepreneur is being able to make your own vacation arrangements!

When I got home and back into the office, it took me a few days to get reentered, if you know what I mean. It is no small thing to go from saris and temples to pantyhose and sales reports. But finally, one day, I got around to asking Hinda where we stood in the patent process and letting her know I was ready to take it back onto my list.

"Oh! No problems, almost done!" she responded to my query.

"Really! What does that mean?" I asked. "They have all the info they need from us now? Let me know so I can get up to speed when I call Roger."

"No need, I'll just keep with it now. It's almost done, you know. We're actually at the filing stage. You don't have to take it back on." Me, being the me I was then, shrugged and said okay.

We were busy; there was plenty to do. I was getting ready for a big trade show, and it was sometime weeks later that Hinda came into my office and put a thick document on my desk. Received from the attorneys, officially stamped, it was a copy of the Jogbra patent *as filed*. I stopped what I was doing and pulled the enormous official packet toward me. To my astonishment, the top line listed the inventor in bold type as: *Schreiber, Hinda S.*

My heart dropped to my feet.

I read on to see my name listed below, then Polly's—neither in bold type. On all subsequent pages of the thick document and elsewhere it would just show "Schreiber, Hinda S., et al." I felt reduced to an "et al." I felt erased, hoodwinked. And, for sure, my ego was bruised.

When I protested, Hinda told me it was a done deal. The patent could not be changed back. It was already filed in the US Patent Office. She handed me our copy. From then on, Hinda's name appears as the inventor of the first sports bra, because most readers miss or skim over the two names following hers—if they are even presented as more than "et al."

Although upset, it was another "effort vs. surrender" wrestle for me, a spiritual conundrum. In fact, because all the paperwork was filed, I had to learn to surrender on this one. And this proved to be the next ingredient in what was fast becoming a major life lesson for me, courtesy of my entrepreneurial endeavor: Between Hinda's position in share ownership and now this order of name-listing issue on the patent, I felt I was being erased—or trying to be erased, made invisible.

Why?

This caused a problem for me that spanned both the emotional and intellectual realms. In private and in therapy, I wrestled with myself: Why should I care? Isn't it just ego, evil ego, that made me care about the patent listing? Or was it okay to feel proud of my achievement in spotting this need and creating a product to meet it? Was it okay to want recognition for this? What about healthy ego and standing up for myself? Certainly, Hinda was instrumental in our business's success—wasn't I just being petty about this patent thing?

One day, a critical conversation took place in the Clarke Street office between Hinda and me. We were in the throes of early success. There had been a flurry of publicity after our debut at the national trade show; journalists were asking us how we got started. They had caught wind of the jockstrap story—it was funny and cute, and it sold newspapers. They wanted to know more.

"Hey Hinda, I saw the article on us," I called to her as she walked by my office door, "great exposure!" Some reporter from the *New York Post* had devoted an entire article to us, a half page with photo. I was sitting in my new office, at my age-old desk.

She stopped and leaned against the doorframe. "Yeah, the guy just called out of the blue. The interview lasted about twenty minutes . . . most of it got in print."

"Great! What was that, though, about how we found a jockstrap in the laundry and that's what gave us the idea? There was my phone call with my sister, y'know. Remember? And don't you remember me telling you about Al coming down the stairs with the jockstrap pulled over his head? Were you on the project by then?"

Hinda didn't reply, just shrugged her shoulders.

"And what about Polly?" I continued. "There's no mention of her. She is, after all, the woman who sewed the two jockstraps together!" I grinned. The story of how things all came together was a great tale. It seemed, however, that Hinda felt differently.

"I think it confuses the story to mention Polly's early involvement," she said from the doorway. "After all, she's not here now. She's in New York doing her costume design thing. It complicates our story; it will just muddy up the waters. For the sake of our PR story—y'know, like Sandage always says—we should keep it simple."

Hindsight, of course, is a wonderful thing. I wish that I could say that it was only in hindsight that I realized what had happened, what was happening. But that is not entirely true. Even in the moment this conversation felt very uncomfortable. I did not want to leave Polly out of the story. For her to remain in it was not only preserving the truth and acknowledging someone for a vital contribution, but it also served to continue what was to me the great story of our antics together, now ongoing and into the public realm of business. ("Friends since junior high turn high jinx into high profits," etc., etc.)

The discussion went on for a bit. I tried to argue for the historical facts. Hinda argued the public relations need for simplicity. I swallowed the disloyalty I felt. Through inaction, I allowed Polly's contribution to become shrouded in the mists of omission.

On the one hand, I could see the point that Hinda was making, but to submit to it was, I felt, the coward's way out. Let me be clear here: not *the* coward's way out— *this* coward's way out. Since finagling ownership of the majority of the shares that I had issued, Hinda had made crossing her opinion or disagreeing with her very contentious and uncomfortable for me. There had been enough screaming fights in the office already. Was this issue worth another one?

What was happening here? What dynamics were at work? My opinion, arrived at much later, was that Hinda felt that Polly's contribution somehow diminished her own role. True, in those very early days, Hinda was not an integral player—it being my idea and direction and Polly's construction talents. But Hinda was the one who got the project off the ground. She found and dealt with the manufacturing. This was no small task. She was instrumental in the Jock Bra becoming the Jogbra and a commercial reality and success! This was a lot to take pride in. Not to mention that her family had loaned us our start-up money. Why did she feel the need to reinvent her role in Jogbra's genesis?

The fact that at that point, very early on, I allowed misrepresentation of the facts to go only weakly challenged—whether it was the "jockstrap found in the laundry" story (which continues to pop up to this day), or more seriously, the issue of Polly's seminal contribution—is painful to me. It is an incident that lived in my heart and my soul as a cutglass example of my imperfection as a being. I know we all do and say things that we are not proud of, but that does not make my own transgression any easier to bear. Polly and I have long since put this tale to rest between us. And in subsequent years, her role has been made known, clarified—she has been interviewed and acknowledged as an inventor of the sports bra. The fact that we are good friends to this day is a blessing. Perhaps the universe is more forgiving than I am.

Early on, Hinda and I had the wisdom to engage the services of a consultant from the organizational development world, David Wagner, who acted as a sort of "couples counselor" for us. Remember, we were always seeking to learn how to do what was needed for our Jogbra baby to thrive, and we were each interested in our own personal growth—so such an action on our part wasn't unusual. It was smart, and brave, and difficult.

Anyway, I believe it was David who first helped us identify the ways in which we both complemented and triggered one another. He gave us some pointers on how we might better get along. David only worked with us for a few months—not long. And it was no magic pill. Our dysfunctional partnership didn't transform overnight. Hinda still would behave confrontationally and raise her voice, and conversely, I would be wounded and unable to find *my* voice. And at that time, there was still the issue of the stock ownership inequity and how Hinda perceived our positions as a result. But we better understood each other's value to the work.

It was around this time that I began to acknowledge to myself that what I only privately thought of as Hinda's "ruthlessness" was useful in the face of my own "softness."

Some would say Hinda was just being smart. Did that make me not smart? What I felt to be her stereotypical male responses to some business situations—competitive, self-promoting, calculating—I found distasteful and did not want to engage those qualities in myself. Thus, we could and often would drive one another crazy. In a very real way, Hinda's opportunistic way of being was a kind of "tough love" solution for ripping away that "nice-girl" cloak I'd been hiding under, a cloak I'd been brought up to believe was also a shield. It was not.

The fact that we could and would agree to the counseling gig with David was in part because, individually, both Hinda and I were also pursuing our own paths to "enlightenment," reaching for our own personal growth. I attribute this in large degree to the fact that my generation was also the "Woodstock Generation," and some of us looked beyond just the music and free love memes into the more cosmic and existential questions that the fast-moving cultural landscape was offering us. In many ways, seeking enlightenment was the "now I'm supposed to" of a certain subset of young adults.

This was, after all, the heyday of the gurus. There were swamis, communes, and meditation camps. On the business side of things, articles on the spirituality of marketing and seminars about how making money need not be a bad thing were appearing. "Sensitivity training" was born. The concept of "business ethics" started developing in academia in the early 1970s and was fully entrenched in the industry by the '80s.

Oh, it was a heady and sometimes confusing time. One might go walk on fire, or sit in silence for a week in India, or meditate transcendentally in your own living room. There was Esalen, Omega, or Kripalu to run away to. It was a time when people who are now respected and acknowledged in the field were just starting out—Richard Alpert morphed into Ram Dass. Tony Robbins appeared. Deepak Chopra left traditional neuroendocrinology medicine to teach Primordial Sound Meditation. Bucky Fuller taught us to think in terms of "Spaceship Earth." And there were so many others. There were programs like EST, TM, Money & You, and Human Factors.

I feel it was almost impossible to be alive then and not be a seeker. And it wasn't as if the rapidly shifting culture was making it easy to simply choose to follow the rules and get on with one's business, gurus and seminars notwithstanding. The "rules," especially for women, were changing. Our "now I'm supposed tos" had shifted away from the traditionally accepted cultural norms, and I was shifting with them.

One hot, summer week I was in Shreveport, Louisiana to work with a sales rep. Going into a rep's home turf was really about helping him become more familiar and comfortable with his sales pitch about bras and the need for a special one for athletics, calling on some of his accounts as part of the process. I wasn't a salesperson really, but I could be passionate about something I believed in, and I was a pretty good teacher; so I didn't sell—I educated.

After our day of appointments, he dropped me off at the single-story, pink stucco motel I was staying in, and I realized I had enough time before dinner to get my run in. I pulled on shorts, T-shirt, shoes (and a Jogbra, of course!) and headed out the door . . . into a totally unfamiliar and unwelcoming area. I was looking at a parking lot off an access road underneath a swooping concrete highway overpass.

I turned and went into the glassed-in front office and addressed the person sitting behind the desk.

"Hey. Hi, there! Can you tell me which way I might go for a jog?"

A man of indeterminate age looked up from the newspaper he was reading. Peering over his wireless eyeglasses he looked me up and down. "A what?"

"Uh, I'm a runner . . . just staying here for the night and don't know the area. Uh, I need a route, a loop or something, just three, maybe four miles that I might run?" The guy just kept staring at me like I was speaking a foreign language. I shifted my weight from one foot to the other. I tried smiling harder.

"Go left out the door," he finally said.

"Should I keep taking lefts?" I asked. "Or just turn around and double back?" He looked at me like I had two heads, shrugged, and returned to his paper. I wasn't smart enough to consider that this might not be such a good idea. I needed a run. I headed out the door, turned left, and simply figured my fail-safe was that I could always just turn around and double back.

As the road to the left unfurled out into undeveloped fields and low, gray-green, Louisiana scrub trees, the traffic all but disappeared. So did any buildings; there was nothing out there. It was just me and the damp, hot southern air, my feet thump, thump, thumping against the dark tarmac. Grateful for this quiet, I ran along the shoulder, listening to my heartbeat and breathing. Until I heard a vehicle coming up behind me.

Out of habit, I shifted off the pavement entirely, onto the grass verge to allow the vehicle to pass safely. It didn't. Nothing was passing me by. Then I heard the sound of an engine being gunned behind me. And a honk. I jumped but kept running. And another honk. And another, longer, insistent. And, though going slowly enough to stick behind me, that truck kept gunning its engine. Finally, I glanced over my shoulder. Right behind me, following at my pace, was a red pickup truck. Crowded in its cab were three men. One was hanging out the passenger-side window, waving something at me. The minute I glanced back at them they all started hollering. Whoops. Catcalls, I suppose. Whatever they were saying I have long since blocked out of my mind.

The perspiration on my body turned cold as fear blanketed me. I did not speed up. I kept my running pace. I did not look at the truck of rednecks again. I just kept jogging.

I don't really know how long they followed me on that lonely road in Shreveport. It was probably only a minute or two before the driver hit the gas pedal hard and screeched on by me, within inches. But it felt like a very long time to me. I noticed the gun rack mounted on the back as they sped off. I tried to read the license plate, but being nearsighted, I couldn't. I spun around and hoped with each step that they wouldn't turn around as well. Fast as adrenaline would take me, I raced back to my pink motel.

12.
OUT AND ABOUT

"You're not selling products. You're creating relationships."
~ Robert G. Allen

Finding the right people and turning an idea into a reality is always a challenge! We had a tiger by the tail. Orders kept coming in, and the learning curve was steep and showing no signs of flattening out. At some point, I came to realize that I was experiencing the consequences of "right product at the right time," but in those early years I had little time to spend reflecting on the phenomenon we had created.

My life in the last two years of the '70s and in the early years of the '80s was all about finding the next, often creative, solution to the current, rising "problem" caused by our unabated growth. And, thanks to Mr. Pickens's excellent phone education about sales reps, I knew finding the right sales representation was key. I was too naïve to know that it might be prudent to open one area of the country at a time. No. Hey! Let's be everywhere all at once.

One major vehicle for reaching potential customers out there was something called "shows"—trade shows and exhibits that took place all over the country. Like most everything else, this was an entirely new aspect of business for us to comprehend, meet, and take advantage of—so we went about doing so.

The granddaddy of these was the one put on annually by the National Sporting Goods Association because it *was* national. Every company came from all over to display their goods, and every buyer came from every retail outlet to see what was new—what new thing, color, or style they might make room for in their budget that year. In February of 1979, the NSGA trade show was to take place in a huge convention center, McCormick Place West, in Chicago. And we were bound and determined to be there. To do so, we needed to be ready with business cards, sell sheets, wholesale order forms, and most dauntingly, a booth. Oh my, I have to laugh as I remember this.

We booked a modest ten-by-ten booth space—the smallest and most affordable available. At first, I wasn't thinking much beyond my old craft-fair days and was envisioning a table with some bras laid out on it. But we'd just hired Sandage Advertising, primarily to do the sell sheets and a mini-catalog ("mini" because we really only had one product in three sizes), and they told us in no uncertain terms that we could not let an opportunity like this big event go by. We had to take advantage of our "real estate" at the show to do some serious promotion. We had to have more than just a table.

It was decided that Hinda, because of her theater background, should be in charge of creating some sort of booth. Her protests that she'd been in *costume* design, not set design or scenery, went unheeded. Now, just to put this in perspective, there are entire companies that design and build trade show booths, but we had no time for this— let alone budget. We only had our cleverness. We'd figure something out.

And so we did—by stretching royal-blue canvas cloth over a frame. We then propped up our "wall" behind our table and pinned our bras up all over it in a fun hither-thither pattern. In addition, a poster-sized picture of a Playboy™ bunny wearing our Jogbra was stationed right alongside our table. Hinda had procured it from the journalist who'd interviewed her for the *New York Post* just a few months before. It turns out the bunny was his girlfriend!

February is cold in Vermont—but it was cold, icy, and windy in Chicago. I recall packing for this event, being nervous about what to wear in my new persona as business owner, seller of jogging bras—*the* Jogbra! While excited about the adventure, I was not particularly at ease about going to a trade show all about sporting goods.

We were a hit. People were standing in front of our booth three deep—and most of them were actually buyers. It was a grand coming-out event!

This turned out to be just the first in a long run of shows we attended. Have I said I traveled a great deal? I mean really, a lot. Those first few years before hiring a full-time sales manager, I was on the road almost every week, and often on weekends, either working with sales reps in their territory or going to some show or another. No small feat for a girl with epilepsy, by the way, wondering each morning if the day will be seizure-free—or not.

My old friend showed up the first day at the NSGA. One morning before the show opened, we had an appointment to interview the Easco sales rep firm, a group of gentlemen who covered the upper Midwest—Michigan, northern Illinois, and Wisconsin, maybe. Because it was a large group—several people as well as Hinda and me—we had arranged to meet in one of the available meeting spaces on the mezzanine level of the cavernous convention hall. There we were, all assembled, when I went down into a grand mal convulsion, falling onto the hard, cold floor. In an effort to be helpful, Hinda forced a ballpoint pen past my lipsticked lips, trying to get it past my tightly clenched teeth. It broke and pierced the skin on my lips, leaving them cut and bruised. Though embarrassed, apologetic, and self-conscious, I recovered from the convulsion, and, as the saying goes, went on with the show—but I had a fat lip for the rest of the trip!

The poor onlookers to that scene! It is frightening for those witnessing a convulsion. I understand that, at first,

I appear just fine, and then in the next moment I'm on the ground, unconscious and jerking my arms and legs uncontrollably and unattractively. It happens so suddenly and appears so violent. It surprises and scares anyone who happens to be around me. Usually, as I return to consciousness a few minutes later and become aware of the concerned faces around me, I struggle through the fuzzy postictal state, as it's called, and start mumbling my apology. "I'm sorry. I'm sorry." At that trade show in 1979, I was no different, spitting the pieces of pen out of my mouth as I struggled to sit up. So self-conscious! It is fortunate that the common wisdom of the time—that one should put something in a seizing person's mouth to prevent them from swallowing their own tongue—is no longer taught or believed. This was the standard thinking back then but, in fact, it is impossible for anyone to swallow his or her own tongue.

We hired that rep firm, and they worked well for Jogbra for many years.

Most of the people working as independent sales representatives in the sporting goods industry in the late 1970s were male—like 99.9 percent. I didn't know this when I started looking for reps. Actually, I didn't even think about gender. I didn't know enough to think about it—not until I caught the first few snickers.

I don't remember which guy in which sales force revealed the first smirk. It was likely at that very first national sporting goods show, which took place in a windy and cold Chicago in the early part of 1979. We met with quite a few sales rep groups during the show, and frankly, we were lucky any of them were interested in talking with us. We had *one* product in *one* color (white) manufactured in three sizes. As I was patiently told later, rep groups typically carried clothing or shoe lines—not single products.

But a few "head reps," the entrepreneurs who pulled together and organized a group of people to create sales in a specific geographical area, were able to see the potential in a bra designed specifically for active women. I made appointments with each group who had responded to my ad, which was pinned up on the exhibitors' bulletin board at the show. Each group would file into our small, ten-by-ten booth either before the show opened or after it closed. The head guy and anywhere from two to five or more "sub-reps" would trail in behind him and, with scarcely concealed nerves that I hoped came off as excitement, Hinda and I would give them the spiel we had worked out.

At that time, sporting goods—especially specialty apparel and shoes—was just taking off. Shoes specifically designed for running were a fairly new phenomenon. New Balance and Nike were hot new brands, and known brands like Adidas and its rival Puma were quick to come out with their versions of both shoes and apparel specifically for running. New companies selling sports-specific clothes were bursting onto the market almost monthly. Tennis stars like Billie Jean King, marathon winners like Bill Rodgers, and big-name football guys were lending their names to these companies and selling their personally branded products.

So, these salesmen were curious. They were wondering, "Who are you guys?" "What's this jogging bra? A *bra*?!" They would talk amongst themselves about whether their retailers would buy it, and if so, which ones. And, of course, they wondered whether they could make money selling it. During the pitch, we would, of course, go over the bra's design and the reasons behind it (based on my original list of problems, herein solved). It was in this part of the sales pitch I first heard a snicker and caught an exchanged smirk. Hey, talking about bouncing breasts and bras was not easy for many men in the late 1970s. I suppose I shouldn't have been surprised.

The only way to deal with it was to do so head on. I would acknowledge any awkwardness, smile, shrug, and then use humor to find a way to, in essence, tell them to get over it. I didn't find it hard to laugh along at the bra and breast jokes, because then I would reiterate: this is a *real* problem, and our product fixes this real problem—it would sell.

I recall catching the eye of one guy who had just smirked at his colleague before glancing guiltily back at me. I looked at him and raised one eyebrow, as if to say, "Really?" And while he did sit up a bit straighter, what really worked for all these guys, and subsequently their retailers, was this simple statement: "The Jogbra is not lingerie; the Jogbra is athletic equipment."

Two important things happened for me after that first round of interviewing and hiring sales reps. First, I learned how to deal with the boyish "bra and breast" responses when they occurred. Second, I started to understand the inherent and very natural advantage that female sales reps would have. Though it opened up questions of reverse gender bias, the fact is, women have breasts and could speak with experience and authority about the problem. The women reps were few and far between, but I found them, and they were *stars*!

We had so much help along the way, so many really capable, lovely people who were our sales representatives across the country, it is almost blasphemous to call out a few individuals. But I must talk about two women.

It was a young man named Angel Martinez—then, just a bright, young guy from Alameda, California, looking to find his path—who helped me find Jan Kimbrell. (Angel would later become a star himself as CEO of Deckers.) Jan repped in Southern California, a key territory in "sales land." And boy, was I learning about that—the differences in sales territories! I had put up a map of the United States in my office and, as I hired rep groups, drew lines around the states (or parts of states) that each group covered. California traditionally was two separate territories: Northern California and Southern California. While both were lucrative, the southern half in particular was considered juicy for sporting goods. Angel gave me Jan's phone number and told me she was the go-to girl for SoCal.

I was nervous about meeting Jan. We spoke on the phone to plan my trip out to meet her and she listed her impressive and long resume in sporting goods, an industry I was only just beginning to grasp. She knew people in this strange world of sporting goods, which she had been a part of "forever," in almost every permutation—buyer, retailer, customer—and now as a manufacturer's sales representative. I also learned she was a native of LA, the land of Hollywood, sun, and beaches. She wasn't so much a runner, she said, more a tennis player, golfer, and surfer. Clearly, she had been one of those girls I had avoided back in school—the ones who excelled in gym and went out for sports.

"Be sure to pack your bikini! We'll hit the beach while you are here," she said before we hung up. *Oh dear*, I thought as I put down the phone, sitting in my cold Vermont office looking at my winter-white skin. I had no idea where my (one-piece) bathing suit might be hiding at this time of year.

On the appointed date and time, I landed at LAX, ready to meet this high-powered, LA/Hollywood glam rep, or so I'd imagined her in my mind—tall and blond, of course, high-heeled and wisp-thin with *perfectly* toned muscles rippling under her *perfectly* tanned, glowing skin.

Well, she *was* blond. And tan. But imagine my surprise when I was met by a woman who might have been from my own preppy girl's school back East: light tweedy jacket, button-down shirt tucked into her pleated skirt, and sensible penny loafers, all on a comfortable, rounded frame—and most welcoming, a ready laugh and sparkling blue eyes with a bit of mischief in them.

Years later, after she had moved to Vermont and become our vice president of sales and marketing, we would compare notes about that first meeting—as well as confess to our own apprehensions and expectations about the other. She'd chosen her preppy look on purpose, of course, in her own anxious anticipation of the unknown East-Coaster coming her way. But she did like the look and would wear it quite a bit, the Hollywood glam thing never being her style. And she recalled breathing a sigh of relief when I cracked some joke right off the bat, and she realized I wasn't going to be some cold, stuck-up New England hard-ass (well, "bitch boss" is what she might have said), and that I knew I didn't know a lot—but wanted to learn.

Jan is a consummate salesperson and a willing teacher. She was very generous and taught me things that at that point I didn't even know I didn't know—such as what a buyer's concerns are, how those concerns differ from one type of outlet to another (chains vs. independents vs. franchises).

How terms of sale may vary, and how they may not. Who owns whom, and why. It all sounds so basic now, but I sincerely had no clue in that first year. Driving to an appointment, Jan would give me the lowdown, and I was a sponge.

And we did go to the beach on that first trip. It was the first of what was to be many beach trips together. Jan had to convince me to get over my pale-skinned self-consciousness. I'd never seen the Southern California beaches before, so beautiful yet so different from those I'd grown up on back East. And, oh my! All those bikini-clad bodies—my uptight, upright Eastern sensibilities got a wake-up call of sorts.

After LA, New York City was the other huge sales territory to be managed, and our sales were not great there. *Why?* we wondered. Because both Hinda and I had lived in Manhattan, and I had family in the area, this was much on our minds. *What was the problem?*

A totally different animal than most anywhere else in the country in every way, NYC needed special attention. Retailers in the city had space concerns, strict profit margins to meet—hence way less risk tolerance. Getting a new product in—let alone something as off-the-wall as a new concept product—was a big challenge. A bra? None of the old-school sales reps who covered the city would touch us.

But once again, a serendipitous turn of events occurred. Malcolm Hetzer was one of the power reps back in those early days. Tall, handsome, and charismatic, he became the center of attention in any room he entered. Mal's rep group covered Northern California, and when I met him, he was carrying one of the fastest-growing shoe lines. After seeing the Jogbra and listening politely to my pitch, he told me candidly he and his guys didn't really have time for our little product. After so sweetly telling me he was too big for us, Mal said, "But I think I have someone who can help you. You don't have anyone in Manhattan, do you?"

I replied that, no, indeed, Manhattan was proving to be a hard nut to crack. He nodded and went on. "My sister, Norine, lives there and is looking to make a career change. Move from Wall Street to sporting goods. She's a dynamite sales person and I think she'd be great for your Jogbra— with a little tutoring from me, of course!" He flashed his gorgeous smile, full of white teeth, and gave me Norine's contact info. Shortly after that conversation, I made the phone call and plans to go down to Manhattan to meet Norine.

Going to New York was like going home again. I'd grown up in and around the city and knew the turf, the hubbub, so I wasn't as nervous about meeting Norine as I had been about meeting Jan. Rather, I was curious, excited, and hopeful about solving the New York problem. When she opened her apartment door, a very large and eagerly friendly golden retriever bounded out into the narrow hallway to greet me. So much for any professional demeanor I had hoped to exude! I leapt back with a shriek and a laugh as the two of us wrangled her beautiful animal back into the apartment.

And so it began. Norine, one of the nicest people I've ever known, was a people person, a natural at selling, and a hard worker. She became one of the top reps in the industry, in one of the toughest and most lucrative territories in the US. And did I say we had fun? So much fun! We traveled together all over the country for one of her accounts. I used to joke that I've been in every mall in the country. Well, not really . . . but it felt that way.

Once a sales representative firm was hired, I would often go and work with one or all of them in their assigned territory. In this manner, I saw a great deal of the United States—well, the inside of malls and sporting goods stores, anyway—and met a great deal of people. Aside from the rep, there were the store's buyer, the salespeople, the merchandiser (if the outlet was large or sophisticated enough to warrant such a position), and, of course, the customers.

Having grown up in my insular, New York/New Jersey, socioeconomic bubble of private schools, yacht club dances, and my mother's particular ideas about her "social circle," this was an eye-opening, "total immersion" learning experience. In retrospect, I have to admit that I had a rather protected childhood, and it was not only because of having epilepsy. The work world I'd experienced prior to Jogbra, while broader (chambermaid, waitress, secretary, artist's model), was still its own bubble, filtered through my married-young, do-gooder, artist's lens. When I went on the road with our sales reps, I felt like I was walking around with my eyes as big as saucers, and my business suit was a costume I was hiding behind.

I knew nothing, had so much to learn. Under the guise of talking about and selling the Jogbra I was getting an education, one that turned out to be not just about the sporting goods business, but really people—about our species, our humanity.

For someone who had experienced such a sheltered and protected upbringing, meeting so many new people from all walks of life was a revelation to me. I met so many people, from all over the country. Not just the sales reps that I traveled with, but the store managers and salespeople on the floor, the customers in the stores, our buyers, and the "vendors" who wanted to sell us things. I met our peers in the sporting goods industry—owners and executives from both new companies like ours as well as those from the old, established concerns.

It was fascinating. Each was a story. The rep from the Midwest who taught me a bit about his Lithuanian heritage; the sub-rep from Stone Mountain, Georgia, who insisted I stay with her and her family while traveling the territory—my very first experience of Southern cooking and a taste of the Southern lifestyle; the other people at trade shows who, like me, would throw off their business clothes, put on running attire, and go off into strange streets of whatever city we happened to be in—we'd hook up in the lobby and go in a small pack. I remember being so intimidated one time because my fellow runner was an ultramarathoner!

One time, I was calling on a big account in Seattle, a catalog account. We had all gathered in their large conference room—me, the buyer, the slightly infamous owner of the catalog, some others on the periphery—when I mentioned that I windsurfed. The owner, Bill, immediately said, "Great! Let's go!" And wham! End of meeting! As he ushered me out of the office, everyone else around the table kind of chuckled and shuffled out, mumbling things like, "Oh, Bill! There he goes again. We'll pick up the meeting when you guys get back, maybe over dinner."

I had to borrow a bathing suit and wet suit (a wet suit!? I was a fair-weather windsurfer!), which were scrounged from a locker room in some strange windsurfing/sports club down on the docks. And what about my hair and makeup afterward? Oh, I was regretting my comment. Then we were on the water, and oh my God! I was really regretting getting myself into this. Windsurfing in the Seattle harbor on a gusty, fall day was like nothing I'd ever attempted on a summer afternoon on Lake Champlain. I was totally out of my league. I couldn't get up or stay up on the large board. The wind was far too strong and the waves too high. I'd never windsurfed in such conditions, though they were seemingly typical for the Seattle crowd. I ended up holding on to the tail end of Bill's board as he raced through the large waves in the brisk western wind. I was totally humiliated.

To my anxious mind in those days, the incident was a travesty. But my "account" didn't seem to mind or notice. He thought I was a good sport for going out, and probably didn't even notice that I no longer had any eye makeup on. And the relationship that developed as a result of that terrible, shared sporting event, and the business we did going forward, was friendly and solid for years to come.

One Sunday, I was in my office on Clarke Street, probably to get ready for yet another upcoming sales trip. I was alone and the doors were all locked. I heard knocking on the back door, out in the shipping area. Once my divorce from Al was truly in the works, I had started seeing someone else. That was odd enough after more than seven years of marriage, but then I actually started dating, seeing more than this one guy—which was tricky, given my work demands and schedule. But hey, this was a new era, right? That's what I was trying to live into, up to.

When I got to the door, I could see through the glass that it was my first post-marriage gentleman friend, owner of the pickup truck that had so annoyed my landlady on College Street. He had been one of the friends who had helped us with packaging and shipping, and had even worked for us part-time early on, before we hired Lydia full-time. I was surprised to see him; we had been having some issues (stemming from me seeing other people) and I hadn't seen him lately. My divorce was just barely being finalized, and I was far from wanting to jump into another exclusive relationship. He was not happy.

And although you could not have told me at the time—I was young and dumb—I opened the door and let him in. He said nothing, just walked determinedly through the shipping area and on into the offices, looking around. I was confused and feeling very awkward, making nervous chatter about how the offices had changed since he'd been there last. When we came into my office, he finally spoke.

"You alone here?"

"Yes . . ."

And he swung and hit me, hard, in the face. I saw, literally, stars and went crashing down onto the thin, brown, industrial carpet.

When I came to, only a few minutes had passed, but I didn't know that then. My attacker had gone. I ran out of the office, looking for him. I was furious. I ran out the back door and down the short driveway looking this way and that. No sign of him.

I got in my car and drove the few short blocks to his apartment. I stopped in the middle of the quiet, tree-lined, residential street and left the driver's-side door open as I launched myself out and stood in front of his building and shouted, "YOU HAVE NO RIGHT!"

Then I called the police.

I didn't see that guy again for years. He left town shortly thereafter and went to Alaska, I heard—in part to escape the sequence of events created when I'd reported the incident to the police, an action several of our mutual friends villainized me for. He was a talented poet; I still have the poems he wrote me. My journals during the time just before this incident are full of admiration for him. Life is never uncomplicated.

But here is the thing: I was angry, and I let it out, big-time. I did not swallow it, stuff it, or redirect it. Unlike my years of inability to confront my husband, Al—who, while never violent, was what might now be called emotionally abusive—I knew that I was not deserving of this extreme behavior and, this time, I acted immediately.

I stood up for myself.

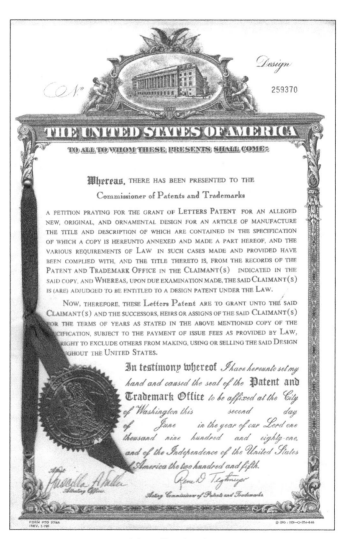

Image of the official Jogbra patent.

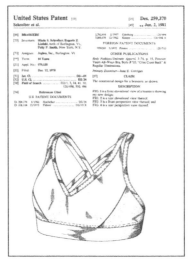

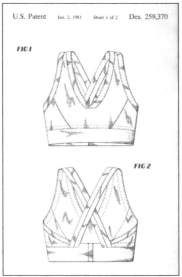

Image of official Jogbra patent drawings.

Our first packaging, which made it easy for
sporting goods stores to display the Jogbra.

Jogbra®.
Why no man-made sporting bra can touch it.

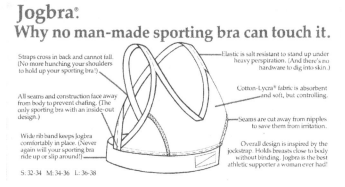

Straps cross in back and cannot fall.
(No more hunching your shoulders
to hold up your sporting bra!)

All seams and construction face away
from body to prevent chafing. (The
only sporting bra with an inside-out
design.)

Wide rib band keeps Jogbra
comfortably in place. (Never
again will your sporting bra
ride up or slip around!)

S: 32-34 M: 34-36 L: 36-38

Elastic is salt resistant to stand up under
heavy perspiration. (And there's no
hardware to dig into skin.)

Cotton-Lycra® fabric is absorbent
and soft, but controlling.

Seams are cut away from nipples
to save them from irritation.

Overall design is inspired by the
jockstrap. Holds breasts close to body
without binding. Jogbra is the best
athletic supporter a woman ever had!

Early package insert showing features of the Jogbra.

Hinda and I (right) sporting Jogbras in an early
sell sheet for sporting goods stores.

Jogbra® in the news.

Jogbra has been written up with enthusiasm in newspapers and magazines.

NEW YORK MAGAZINE extended "a hearty welcome to Jogbra" in its Best Bets column.

The New York DAILY NEWS featured Jogbra in Gearing Up, its weekly consumer sporting goods column that tests new products and advertising claims. Wrote the NEWS: "Four female athletes tested the Jogbra for Gearing Up and all said they would recommend it to any active woman."

With this kind of coverage, you can expect a lot of women to show up in your store asking for Jogbra.

Jogbra was also illustrated and written up in WOMEN'S WEAR DAILY: "One of spring's newsiest offerings is Jogbra's halter construction that takes to the paths in innerwear-outerwear brights."

A new ad campaign is getting Jogbra talked about across the country.

Jogbra is running a new ad that tells active women about the Jogbra's unique history and product features. Ads will appear in sports and women's magazines.

Mat ads and a new merchandising piece help you sell Jogbra in your store.

If you want to run a Jogbra ad, let us know. We will supply a camera ready repro ad to which you can add your own identification.

For large orders, we offer a co-op advertising program.

Our new point of purchase display unit comes with a detachable poster panel that tells the Jogbra story in detail, as well as displaying the Jogbra packages attractively.

It can function like a knowledgeable salesperson, ready to answer the many questions women so often ask about athletic bras.

JOG-79-S004

Early Jogbra collateral marketing piece for sporting goods dealers.

My business card. Logo created by a friend
of Polly's using "Press Type."

Early ad for the Jogbra aimed to dealers.

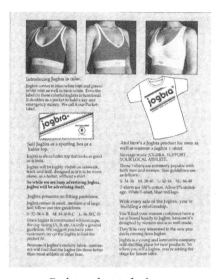

Early product info sheet.

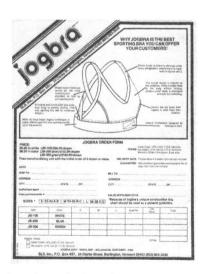

An early Jogbra order form for sporting goods stores.

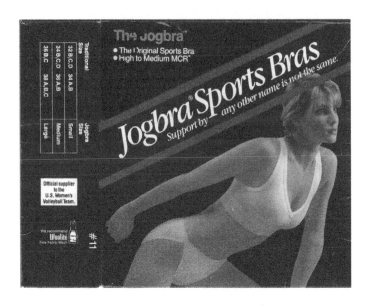

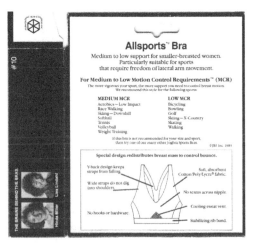

Jogbra becomes Jogbra Sports Bras with sophisticated
new packages (flattened for photography).
Note "The Brains Behinds the Bras" on the side panel.

By Women for Women   Jogbra®Sports Bras

1990s promo piece.

Fooling around after a photoshoot for a very early catalog.

Photo Collage: The Product

The foremost athletic sports bra.

Our famous Jogbra® is soft, cool, and extra supportive. Concealed seams cannot chafe, straps cross in the back so they cannot slip, special ventilating panel placed where moisture collects and double layer front all combine to provide the comfortable support the active woman needs.

- Wide cross-in-back straps
- Extra support front panel
- Cotton poly Lycra® fabric
- No hardware to dig or chafe

SIZES: S, M, L (see size guideline)
COLORS: White, beige

The Jogbra in sporty colors.

All the same great Jogbra® features plus the added versatility of wearing it alone as a halter, as well as under a top.

SIZES: S, M, L
COLORS: Light Blue, Light Pink, Lavender

Our new bra designed for the firmer breasted, all-around woman.

This bra is terrific for juniors and the woman that requires less bra but still wants that lightweight support without chafing. The unique "Y"-back design provides extra support and keeps straps in place. And, like our Jogbra®, it can be worn as a halter-top too!

- Cotton poly Lycra®
- Unique racing back
- Sweat vent cools where moisture collects

SIZES: S, M, L
COLORS: White, Beige, Light Blue, Light Pink, Lavender

Pages from our 1985 catalog.

POINT OF PURCHASE DISPLAYS

Informed salespeople and customers translate into sales.

Our attractive self-standing or hanging plexiglass display units make a handsome presentation for our packaged products, which have the features and the benefits of all our products clearly outlined on each package.

Please ask your sales representative or call our customer service representative to find out how to receive one of our P.O.P. displays free of charge.

support center

SPORTS UNDERWEAR CONT'D	WINTER SPORTSWEAR

Our new brief, designed for the more traditional man.

Like the Sportbrief, our Hipster is an alternative to the conventional jockstrap. Fuller cut over buttocks and hips make this brief suitable for swimming, as well as for tennis, running, or everyday use for the active man.

- Full cut over buttocks
- 3-inch side on hip
- Poly-cotton-Lycra®

SIZES: S, M, L.
COLORS: White, Royal blue, Navy

The exciting product born out of a new need among athletes.

People who do cardiovascular-type exercise outdoors in cold weather get too warm for heavy gloves, but they do need a windbreaker for their hands. Jogmit™ is the answer, keeping out the elements while letting moisture escape.

- Water-Repellent, breathable GORE-TEX™ fabric
- Clip together for fastening to clothes
- New reflective strip across mitt

SIZES: S, M, L.
COLORS: Silver & Navy

All the features of the Jogmit™ with a special fleece lining for extra warmth.

And the deerskin palm creates a no-slip grip for ski poles. The polypropylene fleece lining gives an added warmth, with the Gore-tex® shell providing water and wind protection.

- Gore-tex® outer shell
- Polypropylene fleece inner lining
- Reflective strip across front
- Deerskin palm patch

SIZES: S, M, L.
COLORS: black, silver, navy

Brand extensions include a men's line and the
Jogmit. First a hit, second a miss!

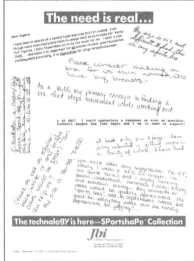

Customers tell us the need is real!

Revolutionary interactive point-of-purchase display piece (front and back) explaining Motion Control Requirements (MCR). The concept is still used today in the industry.

right control for your breasts.

Sportshape™ Bra
For larger-breasted women

Designed for fuller breasted women. Available in traditional bra styling and sizing (cup sizes to 44DD). Sportshape has 100% cotton cup, double layered construction with mesh trim for coolness.

Other Design Features:

- Unique, double layered "baseball cups" for maximum control and minimized profile.
- Adjustable straps and back.
- All hardware plush-lined to prevent chafing.
- Stabilizing rib band won't ride up.

MCR Rating:

High to medium MCR sports, small to large frame.

32-38 B-DD	40-44 C-DD

Available in white and beige.

Lycra Sport Top
With a *real inner bra* of CoolMax/Lycra

Our sport tops have con structed inner bras for maximum control of breast movement.

Other Design Features:

- Racer back for freedom of shoulder movement.
- One-way stretch Nylon/Lycra outer shell for serious control.

MCR Rating:

High to medium MCR sports, medium to large frame.

S	M
32 ABC 34 A	32 C 34 BCD 36 ABC

L	XL
36 CD 38 BC	36 D 38 D

Available in a rainbow of colors.

Cotton/Poly/Lycra Sport Top
With a *real inner bra* of CoolMax/Lycra

Designed with Cotton/Poly/Lycra for the comfort of cotton and the control of Lycra.

Other Design Features:

- Sleek racer back for freedom of shoulder movement.
- Stabilizers in the straps to prevent slipping and stretching.
- CoolMax inner bra wicks moisture away.

MCR Rating:

Medium MCR sports, small to medium frame.

S	M	L
32 ABC 34 A	34 BC 36 AB	36 C 38 BC

Available in lots of great colors.

Cotton Long Top
With a *real inner bra* of CoolMax/Lycra

All the great features of the cotton sport top with long-line styling that covers the midriff for a flattering silhouette.

Other Design Features:

- Cutaway racer back keeps straps in place.
- Stabilizers in straps to prevent slipping.

MCR Rating:

Medium MCR sports, small to medium frame.

S	M	L
32 ABC 34 A	34 BC 36 AB	36 C 38 BC

Available in great colors.

A page from 1980s catalog.

Lisa and Polly, age 14, best of friends. First
selfie! Note pesky bra strap.

Polly with her number one client, Miss Piggy.

Barbara Sandage, Norine Lassa, and I having
brunch at Jan Kimbrell's home in Vermont.

In front of new 13 Ave. D building with staff.

Hinda Miller, Jan Kimbrell, and me.

Success?

Me and Hinda with reproduction of early Jogbra.

A unique "thank you" from Noreen to JBI.

Fashion show, late-80's sales meeting.

Too much fun at our sales meeting skiing event.
(Norine, me and Norine's sister, Ginny Hetzer.)

Hinda, me, and Jan performing "The JBI Rap" at 1989 sales meeting.

More outdoor fun with long-term JBI staffer Sue Janes.

Me in front of our "brag wall" at 13 Ave. D.

My office, 13 Ave. D.

Norine Lassa and I having fun on Lake Champlain.

Snapped at a personal appearance at Bloomingdales.

13.

WHO'S WORKING
FOR WHOM?

*"In the 20th century women will change the nature of power
rather than power changing the nature of women."*
~ Bella Abzug

We were growing an average of 25 percent per year and were profitable almost every year. We didn't know that was unusual, but it was. To me, at any rate, it simply meant we were getting a good "report card."

Our corporate structure was changed to better reflect what we had become. Part of "Entrepreneurship 101" was learning about C corporations versus Subchapter S corporations versus all other permutations of corporate entities. Legal firms were happy to help us navigate through all this.

Our corporate name changed as well. Gone was SLS, Inc. Gone was the brief foray as Jogbra, Inc. Ultimately, JBI, Inc. was born, and it stuck. This was always a bit of a nonsensical name to me, as in my mind the "JBI" stood for

"Jogbra Inc.," meaning we were now "Jogbra, Inc., Inc." It was redundant, but making sense was never a prerequisite of naming the corporate entity, right?

Though we had started with them in South Carolina and remained with them for several years, it wasn't long before our growth outstripped Active Manufacturing's ability to keep up with us. We could not continue having them as our only facility. We had to figure out how to be less dependent on one factory and what to do next. Who could make enough Jogbras to meet the demand?

Placing an ad in *Women's Wear Daily* yielded our answer. Actually, we only had one answer to our ad, but thank heavens it was the right answer. It gave us a major player in our new universe: Mel, and his factory in Puerto Rico.

I ended up leaving this relationship to Hinda. First, because that end of the business, while necessary, did not interest me—and since establishing our working relationship with Active Manufacturing, she had been handling the production end. I was grateful to her for doing so. And second, because upon meeting Mel, I felt uncomfortable. I'm not sure why, but he struck me as untrustworthy, though I had nothing but my gut upon which to base this reaction. Hinda, on the other hand, got along quite well with Mel. In fact, I believe this became an important relationship for her.

Remember, we were both like sponges—soaking up everything we could in order to learn how to run our business efficiently. But it was more intense than the sponge meta-phor implies—it was more like learning how to ride a thor-oughbred racehorse in the middle of the Kentucky Derby. And getting thrown off the horse was not an option for either of us—we wanted to see it through. We didn't even know what the end might look like at that point. Back then it was one day, one sale, one shipment at a time.

Hinda was a willing student when Mel took her un-der his experienced wing and taught her all about garment manufacturing. In short order, Hinda and Mel became close. She felt he was a mentor. Eventually, she even came to know his family in New York.

It was on one of the rare occasions that I was at the factory in Aguas Buenas that something occurred to so-lidify my initial distrust of Mel. The three of us—Hinda, Mel, and me—were sitting in the factory's small office dis-cussing some aspect of our still new working relationship and contract with him. The factory was a low, single-story concrete building with an open floor plan. Mel's office was the only closed off, discrete space and was located right off the main floor of the factory. The atmosphere was hot and humid. The rows of humming sewing machines, each captained by a woman "operator," sat on the gray concrete floor on the other side of the thin office wall. There was a sliding glass window in the wall so Mel could see out onto the floor.

The factory was its own universe. Once the "raw materials" arrived—the fabric, thread, and elastic—they went to the cutting room, where they were cut according to the patterns we had designed and provided. At the beginning of Jogbra's history, this was still being done by hand, by a person whose profession was the "cutter." Precision and layout were key. Fabric waste—what lay outside the patterns and fell to the cutting-room floor—was a key expense that could only be controlled by the cutter's judgement, expertise, and care. As time and technology progressed, this became automated, computerized. Precision became less of a worry. But back in the day, cutting stretchy elastic and fabric was no easy task. It was an art, a specialized skill. Having a good "cutter" was very important to the overall operation. Then, once cut, a bundle of particular pattern pieces would go to each operator.

Each "line" of sewing operators had a function—one might sew in a label, while another would attach the rib band to the cup section, and yet another line of operators was responsible for only sewing on the straps. A garment was built using these separate operations. No one person sewed an entire bra. I'd learned that the labor portion of a garment was priced by how many separate operations it took to put it together. The fewer operations, the less it costs. The more complicated, the more sewing operations, and the more it costs. Such was cut-and-sew subcontracting. And it influenced the design of a garment.

There I was in what was for me a very alien world, in the trenches of the garment industry. Who would have thought!? I didn't think my "Princess Grace" schtick would play here at all. In the office, Mel's big, old, gray metal desk took up most of the space. We sat perched on folding chairs in front of it; I got that functionality was all that mattered in a factory. In the middle of our discussion, Mel suddenly got up and left, telling Hinda and me to continue and that he would come back in a bit. He went out onto the floor and disappeared between the rows of sewing machine operators. I can't recall what Hinda and I began speaking about. I do remember feeling confused, not understanding what was going on at that moment, why Mel had left. I got up and started pacing while we talked, as I am wont to do. I noticed Mel's desk drawer was open and saw a slight movement within. I did a double take, then moved closer. There was a small tape recorder inside. Its reels were going round and round. Were we being taped? Astonished, I pointed it out to Hinda. She said nothing, just shrugged.

I sat down, utterly shocked. What had we been saying? Was there something Mel hoped we would say privately that we would not say while he was in the room? What? I honestly had no idea.

"What, the fuck?" I asked Hinda, using a word I very rarely employed. She shrugged silently. We sat in tense silence, rather awkwardly I think, until Mel returned. When I asked him why he had a tape recorder going in his drawer,

Mel shrugged, flashed a big smile, and mumbled something. He reached in, turned off the tape machine, and slammed the drawer shut. Nothing more was said about it, and the conversation returned to production issues—inventory levels, quality controls on raw materials, the number of bras per week we were willing to commit to his factory. Routine business talk. But I was left with a new and disconcerting thought: Where did my business partner's allegiances lie?

I'm sure we came to some agreement during that visit. We likely all had dinner in town before I went back to Vermont as scheduled, leaving those unfamiliar waters behind.

In great measure, I left production and that part of the business to Hinda and her team and was happy to be able to do so. Production was a difficult, complex aspect of the business. It was not easy to predict how many of each size and color bra were going to be needed within a certain timeframe. And the lead time! We had to order our raw materials far ahead—sometimes weeks, more often months—from fabric and elastic vendors while also allowing for their shipping times. Once the materials finally arrived at the factory, they had to be inspected. If their quality met our established standards, the cut and sew orders would be put into action. These orders were based on our sales and incoming ordering trends. Only then, maybe, hopefully, several weeks later, we would get a batch of inventory completed and over to our warehouse, where it might take us several days to inspect, package, and ship. It was an elaborate, continuous cycle. Production was a central and expensive part of our business and the resultant inventory was the bulk of our assets. As such, it had the potential to, quite literally, put us under, if mismanaged. Over the years, I would routinely thank God for Hinda and our excellent production team.

At one point early on in our relationship with the factory in Puerto Rico, it became apparent that we were fast becoming inventory rich and, as a result, cash poor. While our sales were increasing dramatically, the number of bras we were being required to order from Mel (to keep "his girls," the sewing machine operators, working steadily five days a week) was increasing at an even faster rate. After a few months of this, our cash flow was all tied up in bras sitting in our warehouse, while even more inventory was being created. Whenever I would question the bills from Puerto Rico and our increasing inventory levels, Hinda would become nervous and defensive, reiterating the factory's need to keep a certain number of sewing lines going. According to her, we *had* to keep building the inventory and paying Mel. Hmmm? Was Mel working for us, or were we working for him? I became frustrated, even frightened, enough so as to ask Hinda this question directly. It did no good.

My attempts to persuade Hinda to negotiate a different deal with Mel continued to fall on deaf ears. She just didn't seem to believe me about how serious our situation was becoming. We had other bills to pay. There was more to our business than just fabric and manufacturing. I guessed she felt pressured—between a rock and a hard place. My inability to correct this scenario created a lot of anxiety in my world; I felt helpless and was at my wits' end. What would it take to make Hinda understand how serious the situation was? Why did what Mel said to Hinda carry so much more weight than what I, her business partner, said?

I struck upon a solution. This was not just my concern; I had become worried about our inventory levels because others had pointed the problem out to me, explaining the hazards as soon as the problem started appearing in our financials. If Hinda wouldn't take my word for it, what would happen if she heard it from the proverbial horses' mouths? I arranged a meeting with our accounting firm and consultant. It was a bit of an ambush, but I was desperate. If she wouldn't believe me, then perhaps she would listen to these experts about the dangers of building up too much inventory for too long. It worked; she listened.

I believe Hinda learned sometime later that Mel was willing to work with us—an unknown start-up with a relatively limited production schedule—because he had filed for bankruptcy the year before and no one else in the industry would touch him at that point. In fact, we were a big part of his road back to solvency, a way to keep his factory alive.

Although Mel was a blessing in the long run, his needs in those early days and our naïveté almost put us under. And Hinda—in her gratitude for Mel's willingness to take us on and teach her so much about the production end of our business—almost refused to see it. It was odd and confusing to me. Why would she so easily and blindly trust a vendor and not listen to me? I realized that this concern went beyond my need to "be liked." This was something else. Finally, I recognized it as dismissal, as not being taken seriously. Those old, familiar behaviors, which I so disliked and to which I had reacted so negatively as a child, were now coming at me from my business partner. It was an underlying dynamic that continued to fuel the existing tensions between us.

The longer we worked together, the clearer it became that Hinda and I had very different operating credos. Perhaps, naïvely, I had bought into my mother's "do unto others as you would have them do unto you" principle. It made sense to me. In my then current New Age–ness, this translated neatly into my ideas of karma, do-gooding, and, of course, being *liked*.

Hinda did not trust me at all. To this day, I do not know why. In a conversation recently, I asked her why, all those decades ago, she had chosen to treat me like an adversary right off the bat, rather than like a friend, a partner. Why, I asked, hadn't she trusted me? After some thought, she simply replied that she didn't know about trust or friendship. Baffled by that response, I inquired further if she had experienced trust in her birth family, thinking of her close relationship with her father. She thought awhile and responded that her family had all done a lot of skiing together. Honestly, I didn't know what to make of this response to my question and didn't pursue it further. I do think Hinda was surprised—and has remained so—that after all the issues Jogbra created, Polly and I have always remained close friends.

Once, in the Jogbra heydays, when I had whined back at Hinda's angry presence and accusatory tone, "Why don't you trust me?" She responded, with much energy, "Trust isn't given, it's earned!" Another time, when I used the term "fair" regarding a transaction, she responded, "Fair has no place in business!"

I was dumbfounded. It seemed to me that my business partner's credo was, "Get the other guy's, before he gets yours!" I had no idea how to deal with Hinda's apparent worldview as she repeatedly expressed it to me in our years together. Hinda's behavior toward me seemed to contrast drastically with her engaging public persona. On one hand, she had all the New Age language down pat, believed in the pursuit of one's personal growth, and actively practiced yoga. Yet with me, she was, well—just mean. This great dichotomy in professed values versus my experience was a constant source of confusion for me during our partnership. I found myself trying to make her change, be different, behave differently toward me. *Like* me! I recently came across an article that, finally, shed some light on this for me. From Eve Tahmincioglu, award-winning labor and career columnist for msnbc.com and the voice behind the popular CareerDiva.net blog, I gleaned the following:

> A 2007 study by the Workplace Bullying Institute found that 37 percent of the US workforce reported being bullied at work. Among those who mistreat their co-workers, women were more likely to target other women (71 percent), compared men who bully other men (54 percent.) 'It's a dirty little secret among women that we don't support one another,' said Susan Shapiro Barash, who teaches gender studies at Marymount Manhattan College, author of 'Tripping the Prom Queen: The Truth About Women and Rivalry' and 'Toxic Friends: The Antidote for Women Stuck in Complicated Friendships.'

Barash goes on to say that she believes this is in part due to our living in what is still a male-dominated society, where women feel there's not enough to go around, that they are excluded—which in turn feeds jealousy and resentment among women who feel like they are fighting for a smaller piece of the pie. I recognized, finally, where my partner's need to compete with me might have come from.

The article finished with a statement that resonated with me; I saw glimpses of those two struggling young women who were growing themselves, changing the world with a bra. It helped me understand that I was not alone, that we were not alone, and it was comforting to know that we were both just trying to cope. To go a little further. Just. A. Little. Further. This is the statement:

> 'We are not taught to manage those emotional experiences within ourselves,' she explained. 'So, as we age, culturally our anger is not taken seriously, so we have two choices: We can turn anger against ourselves, and that's where we see eating disorders, self-mutilation, any kind of addictive behavior like shopping or substance use. Or it turns outward with hostility, undermining, biting behavior towards other women.' (Joan Rosenberg, a psychologist and co-author of *Mean Girls, Meaner Women*.)

I turned my anger inward, my business partner turned hers outward. And together, ironically, the sum of these two parts helped create positive change in the world for all women.

It became apparent to me that this idea of working for myself was a sweet and rather naïve illusion. In retrospect, I wonder why this did not become crystal clear to me the moment I signed a personal guarantee to the bank for $100,000. It was probably because I had no sense of owning anything of value at the time. It did not occur to me that I wasn't working for myself—at least not until this was pointed out to me by our very astute consultant, Dick Kohler. Using his wry sense of humor and actual (and extensive) experience in business, he taught me so much. It was he who asked me, "You realize you are really just working for the bank, don't you?"

I didn't. Not then. Not until I thought about it, and about that $100,000 guarantee I had so blithely signed.

So, who were we working for—or with—and why?

We did not work for Mel. He worked for us—or so I thought at the time. Was I just working for myself? For the bank? For my business partner, the majority shareholder at that point? For our customers, to get them the product they needed and wanted?

Eventually, I came to understand that we were all working for each other. It was another lesson learned. The importance of relationships was again revealed, as was the nature of finding the correct balance in order to nurture interdependence.

Our biggest discretionary expense was advertising and marketing. Just as Mel was a mentor and tutor for Hinda on the production side, Barbara Sandage of Sandage Marketing was a mentor for me. And I was fertile ground.

Being an artist and a writer for most of my life and having grown up watching my father work his marketing magic, I was primed for work on this aspect of the company. As noted earlier, Barbara was a powerful personality and an anomaly for working women of the time. As she was an ace manipulator, at times it was difficult to ascertain who was working for whom. But really, that is unfair. I believe Barbara always had Jogbra's best interests at heart, even as she kept her company's interests in sight. But just as I was a tad suspicious of Mel, there were times Hinda seemed nervous and a bit suspicious of Barbara or her motivations.

It was under Barbara's tutelage that we moved from plastic bag packaging to a sleek, glossy black box, evolved from one logo to another, and came up with our ad campaigns and showstopping sales meeting routines. Her firm worked with us for over a decade, right up through our sale to Playtex™.

I've said it before, and I'll say it again: in the end, we are all working for each other.

14.

HITS AND MISSES

"It's fine to celebrate success but it is more
important to heed the lessons of failure."
~ *Bill Gates*

There were many reasons for our initial decision to size the Jogbra in only small, medium, and large. First, the design naturally lent itself to this simplicity. Second, our first major distribution channel—independent sporting goods stores—could not and did not want to carry a large array of stock-keeping units that "traditional" bra sizes would require. The landscape (breast-scape?) of 32A through 40DD and more was staggering in terms of the retail real estate it demanded. This mirrored our own very real concerns about inventory investment, planning, and controls.

Being an entirely new product with virtually no selling history made predicting how particular sizes would sell truly a crapshoot. When I was doing the initial planning, it wasn't even possible to rely on regular bra sales history—those were in decline. It did not even cross my mind to look at regular bra sales. So, only dealing with three sizes was more doable—and infinitely more saleable to our initial primary distribution channel.

But that first Jogbra was built on my frame. I am five foot six, medium-boned, with ample breasts. When I was running thirty miles a week, my ultraskinny running weight was one hundred twenty-seven pounds. Early feedback we got on our original Jogbra was that it was "too much" garment for some. The women with this complaint were generally more petite or had smaller breasts. So, it was clear we needed to have another bra—one for petite, smaller-breasted women, a scaled-down version of our original. Regarding colors, we added beige early on, learning from our customers that it was actually more popular than white. More, and too often poor, color choices came later: Green! Blue! Stripes! We were thinking sporty...Uh, no! Not back then.

At the same time, we were also receiving notes from women asking, "Can I wear this? I don't jog. I play tennis/squash/walk/do aerobics (fill in any nonrunning sport). But this looks so comfortable. Can I wear Jogbra anyway?" We realized the limiting factor of our name "Jogbra" and that some people took it quite literally.

In response, we made another mistake.

We developed the smaller, lighter, scaled-down version of the Jogbra. This was not the mistake. But when it came time to give this product a name, we thought we would kill two birds with one stone, as the saying goes, and call it the "All-Sports Bra." We'd meet the needs of the smaller woman and have a bra whose name wasn't limited to "running." That was the mistake, as this style was so not for *all* sports. For one, it was not as supportive as the Jogbra, having less coverage.

This was all happening very early on, maybe early 1980. We were still learning about the nature of breast support. At the time, there were few, if any, studies being done. Later, of course, this would become an area of study that we actively supported (pun intended). And to this day there are sports medicine people who specialize in breast motion.

And so we launched our second product and had the beginnings of a line of sports bras. In those early years we got off track quite a bit. But we were learning. We were learning the importance of not being a one-product company. And learning of the different support needed by women, because we were hearing from them. We began hearing feedback right away but taking action on any of it had to wait until the Jogbra (style #101) was on her way.

Eventually we came out with a bra to wear under leotards—aptly named the Leotard Bra. Next, there was the SportShape for larger-breasted women, and all in a variety of colors. The line evolved over time. Some products came and went, while others became staples. And some . . . some just should have stayed on the drawing board.

Mistakes—we made some doozies. I got to the point where I expected them and would pad the budget knowing something would blow up somewhere and need a cash bandage. Especially when it might be unforeseeable and out of our control, like a flaw in some raw material that went unseen in the factory and was sewn up into our product. Then our quality control team would spot it and the whole lot would become "seconds" (below standard quality products). We'd have to mark down this inventory, which would negatively impact our revenue. Although we had learned to plan for a certain number of seconds, it was a difficult to accurately predict.

More often, we'd just make a bad decision—like, "Let's have Kelly-green Jogbras! Sure, *they'll* sell!" Oops! More markdowns! Each year, there was always something that hit our bottom line in some surprisingly detrimental way. I got to the place of just hoping it was a *small* something.

And while we all know now that mistakes are learning opportunities, does everyone also know that boredom is probably the number one reason entrepreneurs go down an errant path?

That's been my experience, anyway. I remember Barb Sandage having to tell both Hinda and me about twenty times that no, we could not, must not, change our logo yet again . . . or our packaging . . . or *whatever* it was, just because we were bored with it. We might see our logo every day, but most of our customers and would-be customers did not.

Jogbra needed, she kept reminding us, to become familiar to them. We needed to build our brand. We did not need to change the logo/packaging/font/whatever just because we were sick of it. There were good reasons to make such changes, but our boredom with how something looked was not one of them. Or—far more extensive and expensive—introduce a new product because we were no longer feeling challenged with what was already in our repertoire.

In our attempts to stay interesting, stay relevant, and meet our customers' needs, we developed some sports bra ideas and styles that never made it further than our design tables—and shouldn't have. I do remember one, though, that did shine for one brief instant. It was called the "Thermobra." I forget what it looked like, but I just can't forget that name! Perhaps the Vermont winters were infiltrating our collective brain.

Our real learning opportunities came not from these mostly reasonable line extensions of more types of bras, but when we branched out into different product *categories*.

Mittens. "Jogmitts" we called them. I kid you not. Leotards. (Well, they did have built-in breast support.) Legwarmers. (They went with our leotards, right?)

These valiant efforts at product diversity took place in the early 1980s. I think we were doing this because even though our sales revenue kept climbing, we were worried about how long the bra sales could continue to increase (oh, little did we know!) and felt that with the advent of these new product categories the growth would continue—and so it did. But our profits, which we were always careful to retain at a reasonable rate, began to erode dramatically. Sales were going up, but profits were going down. A year after their introduction, it was apparent that the new products were not contributing to our bottom line. Analysis revealed that our old "standards," specifically the Jogbra, were carrying our new products. When broken down, it became clear that it was costing us money to make this other stuff. Such stuff had to go.

Cutting products from the line was a painful decision, but it was a huge lesson for me. Being a visual learner, it was eye-opening to see the shift on the profit and loss statements. The deletion of those off-niche product categories had an immediate impact on our bottom line. For the first time in our history, the yearly sales revenue fell below the previous year, but our profits shot back up. *Hmmm.*

Of course, we went on to introduce new products, but lesson learned: they were line extensions, variations on our sports bra theme, of which we were the undisputed leader. We were much more cognizant of our niche. We were aware of economies of scale. We kept growing and learning, growing and learning.

And along with our misses were our hits.

There are two ways to support the breast: encapsulation or compression. The former is what traditional bras have been doing for decades—holding the breast in a cup suspended from the shoulders and shaped to conform with fashionable styles of the times. In the 1950s, bras were pointy, almost bullet shaped. In the 1960s, the pointy look gave way to a more natural shape, thank heavens, and we were told it was good to "lift and separate." Compression was the other option—basically using the chest wall as support by smooshing the breast tissue against it, minimizing the pull gravity could have on its mass. Women with larger breasts were familiar with this method. In fact, there are bras to this day that are designed to have "minimizer" cups, which encapsulate *while* smooshing.

We heard from this group of larger-breasted women soon after news of our Jogbra hit the streets. Our inaugural style #101 was not doing an adequate job for them. They needed more support than our cupless version of compression could give them. Finally, when we were able, we waded into the sophisticated waters of traditional, structured cupped-bra design in order to address their needs. And, as Polly had predicted in those very early days, it was a challenge.

We knew that this was a specialized field and that we were going to have to confer with actual bra designers. We hadn't done this before—another benchmark. It turned out there were, in fact, freelance bra designers for hire, so we married our expertise of an active woman's needs with the engineering know-how of a for-hire freelance bra designer. After a lot of trial and error, we came up with a workable solution. In this style, the cup—in order to accommodate the greater tissue mass—had to have seams. This was a problem, so we placed them above and below the nipple to best avoid chafing. And because it rather looked like one, we dubbed it the "baseball cup." We were not without humor.

Because manufacturing, garment and otherwise, still existed in the US back in the mid-1980s, we tried to locate domestic manufacturing for this style, which we were calling the SportShape. But try as we might, the lowest cost we were bid was what we could sell it for if we made it overseas. That meant the US-quoted cost was roughly 100 percent more than what the overseas company quoted us, even with shipping costs included. What a dilemma! Do we hire US workers but then need US customers to pay twice the amount for our product? Or do we use a reputable Hong Kong firm and give US customers the same product for half the price? This was just one of the many ethical issues I had to ponder in the wild, wild ride of turning an idea into a reality that decided not just to manifest, but to manifest *big* and *fast*.

As we added new bra styles, it became apparent that we needed to clarify the differences between our products for our consumers. We now had the original Jogbra, (created on my frame, primarily for running), the All-Sports Bra, the Leotard Bra, and the SportShape Bra.

One day, I was in the cosmetics area of some large department store, probably zoning out between business appointments. We called this "retail therapy," and back then it was still an effective option for me. On this occasion, I noticed a skincare company that had a manually interactive display at their counter. It asked me to indicate my hair color and my eye color. It then recommended a foundation color for me. I don't wear foundation, but I was just playing, passing time. I had a huge *aha!* moment. I looked at the little skincare indicator in front of me and thought, *We need this for our bras.*

As soon as I arrived back in Burlington, I went to Sandage Marketing and explained my idea. How could we convert my *aha!* into a real point-of-purchase sales tool? Our "Motion Control Requirements" chart and wheel was born, even though this was just the beginning of any mechanically—let alone scientifically—measured movement of breasts during activity. Such studies, if they were being done at all, were most likely conducted in basements by grad students. The published papers, the legitimacy of such studies, would come later.

Sometimes, we were still forced to convince people (usually not women) that breast movement was even a problem. Nonetheless, it was really just a matter of common sense: some activities made the breasts move more (causing greater discomfort) than others. As a result, some garments had to deliver greater motion control than others. This was the main reason why we had created more than just one style of bra. As the inventor and the sports bra authority, the Jogbra company had to make a statement about motion control requirements. Hence the Motion Control Requirements Chart—and its interactive point-of-purchase display, the MCR Wheel—was born.

I wish I had patented that one! It lined up bra size, sport, and our sports bra styles to show which would deliver the appropriate support. Brilliant, if I do say so myself.

November 1988, my fortieth birthday. I decided one way to celebrate was to go to Hong Kong and China to see the factories we were using there to make our more traditionally designed SportShape Bra. What a good decision! The experience blew my mind. Here's an observation from my journal from the time:

> Teeming modern city with patches of rural life tucked amongst the neon urban congestion. Forty-story high-rise apartments . . . all have balconies on which, even in the poorest sections, there are an abundance of potted plants and palms. Also—very funny to see—laundry hung out to dry, forty stories up.

I ate eel, snake, and ricebird (very small, eaten whole—beaked head and all) and other culinary delights. It all tasted good: *han ho, ho sac* (very good, good to eat). It is ironic that I went on this trip harboring an express dislike for what I thought of as "Chinese food," only to discover that no food there even remotely resembled its American version. The vegetables were fresh and delicious, the fish beyond compare, the seasonings exquisite. My, how I raved on about the food! I was just so astounded at the difference between my expectation and the reality.

I found the Hong Kong people to be very touch oriented. They were always taking your arm, touching your back, even holding your hand as you walked along. Very nice. They were also very family oriented. Families lived together—grandparents, parents, children, in-laws. For members of the same family to have separate homes seemed very odd to my Chinese Hong Kong associates. Perhaps accordingly, nepotism was the norm in business there. It was who you knew that was important. Anything could be accomplished with a phone call or wave of a hand if you knew the right person. People didn't just work together in Hong Kong, they ate, played, and vacationed together as well.

I learned shopping was a way of life, a legitimate Hong Kong pastime. Anything and everything could be bought or sold, and there were all sorts of ways to shop—local markets, vendors in stalls along certain streets, high-end boutiques.

The elite boutiques were like those one might find on Rodeo Drive or Fifth Avenue, only in Hong Kong they were not located in one place, but rather scattered like copious confetti all over the city. And between these two extremes—the markets and the boutiques—was the whole gamut of storefronts. These could be reputable or not. There was really no way to know, except to judge the merchandise with your own eye—and check the arithmetic on the bill when you dared to buy. And lest I forget to mention it, the price on a price tag had nothing to do with what you would end up paying, except perhaps as a starting point for negotiations. Bargaining was a way of life there.

And the games! Everyone seemed to love games: cards, horse racing, mah-jongg. I think the retail bargaining was just another expression of fun competition. All the games seemed to have an aspect of gambling. Everything was played for money, at least among my colleagues there. They were surprised and delighted to learn that I liked to play games as well. This knowledge resulted in quite a change, creating a greater degree of comradery. They offered to teach me one of their favorite card games, a form of poker, and their natural formality seemed to drop away. They were pleased, I believe, that they did not have to alter their regular after-dinner card game ritual during my visit—I just joined in!

My last two travel days were spent in the People's Republic of China, visiting our Hong Kong factory's extension there. Being in China was a thrill. It seemed to exist in another time, a different universe unto itself. To get there, we took a train to the border, where we went through China's scary and intimidating customs process. I was thankful to be with Chinese friends. A car met us at the border, and we drove two and a half hours to Dongguan. When I say "we" I mean my colleagues from the Hong Kong factory, who also operated this factory in China. Andy, the *tai pan* (or boss); Waitz, a woman who was his top assistant; Kim, her assistant and the Chinese factory's main man, who I only knew as Honey-Bunny; and the driver, who ate with us at every meal. In a gray and drizzling rain, we drove through rice, sugar, and banana tree fields. Going through a village of mud roads, rough wooden buildings and lean-tos used as dwellings, I saw a man cooking on a wok over an open flame in an alley outside.

At Jogbra, we would refer to it as "Andy's factory," but actually the factory there was a joint venture between Andy and the "work unit" of his hometown, Dongguan. Someone told me that he had been a high school basketball star, being tall by Chinese standards. He left "before the war" (the Cultural Revolution of the late '60s) and came to Hong Kong, where he learned English in night school. Now that he could return to Dongguan to do business, he liked to play the *Tai Pan* (or "big boss") to the hilt.

When we reached the factory, I was impressed. It was a large, square, no-nonsense building standing in a dirt field.

Clearly, it was brand new construction. Inside, it revealed the kind of cleanliness that prompts the phrase, "You could eat off the floor." I looked closely at the lines of sewing operators, all women. Only a few would meet my glance, and then shyly. But I noticed that their eyes were bright, clear. I didn't detect shadows lurking there, and I realized something in me was relieved.

The hotel I stayed in, The White Swan, was luxurious and elegant. Built expressly, I guessed, for visiting Western capitalists like myself and our in-country colleagues. It had many treasures of China's past displayed in its spacious lobby area: four-foot-high fine porcelain ginger jars; tall, intricately carved jade statues; lacquered furniture; and silk screens were scattered throughout. A life-size peach tree, dripping with ripe fruit peeking out from its greenery, stood in one corner and caught my attention. Only upon closer inspection did I realize that none of it was real—it was all carved entirely from jade.

My questions about and exclamations over the beauty of The White Swan's historical décor prompted personal stories from my new friends about their lives during the Cultural Revolution—the tragedies, humiliations, losses. I thought about how all these beautiful examples of China's long history had survived the Cultural Revolution and ended up here, to delight visitors. Somehow, once reviled, they had transformed into now being politically correct, a nod to the people's cultural esteem.

It is so trite, but so true: if we do not remember history, we are doomed to repeat it.

Earlier in the 1980s, we had graduated from our plastic bag packaging to a more sophisticated cardboard box. Black, glossy, with our new JBI logo, it worked well with all the other packaged goods in the industry and afforded for more merchandising opportunity, offering photos of the bra, diagrams, etc. It was on this box that the "brains behind the bras" headshots of Hinda and me first appeared.

The new JBI logo had been born not just because of whatever internal corporate structural shuffling was going on, but also to accommodate what was coming . . . our men's line.

Equal opportunity! Turnabout is fair play! Men are people, too!

You'd have thought we would have learned our lesson: stay in your niche! However, I cannot say that our introduction and addition of a line of men's athletic underwear was a mistake. It was not; it was another hit. Over the years, we'd been getting numerous requests from men asking us to do for male athletes what we had done for the female athletes. Men wanted us to make sports support comfortable for them, too. Lord knows—both sexes knew—the traditional jockstrap was not a comfy item to wear.

So, finally, we did. Using thoughtful performance fabrications—some of which were the same we had researched for our women's line—we created "Max for Men." By now "performance fabrics" were coming into their own. This was the era when the fabric industry was getting reinvigorated through technology. New performance-enhancing materials were becoming available all the time.

We did our informal research, talking to all our athletic male friends and colleagues, our key sales reps and their accounts. In essence, the first Max product was simply a streamlined tighty-whitey sort of brief made with a comfortable, four-way stretch material without the need for a front opening. It was comfortable, supportive, and sexy. No straps. And it came in sporty colors that guys liked.

This was the era when Jockey™ caused a bit of a media frenzy by putting Jim Palmer, the handsome Baltimore Orioles pitcher, in ads wearing only their Elance™ brief. Hot! We found our Jim Palmer version (locally, no less) and did similar photography showcasing Max.

Our basic product was soon followed with the "Power Liner," a garment now known as "compression shorts," that provided support and muscle warmth down to the top of the knee. This also was a big hit. Now, you can see them everywhere, on all genders.

Max was a success. Our reps could pull it out of their bag right along with the Jogbra. Our dealers had come to trust us and were willing to try our new products. They understood and embraced the concept of Jogbra introducing sports underwear for men. There was a bona fide need for men's sports support to be revamped. Our reps and dealers anticipated, as did we, that our Jogbra wearers would buy Max for the men in their lives—and many did.

Women creating men's underwear. Again, the irony was not lost on me.

15.

GROWTH AND
PERSONAL POWER

"More than once in the history of Whole Foods Market, the company was unable to collectively evolve until I myself was able to evolve—in other words, I was holding the company back. My personal growth enabled the company to evolve."
~ John Mackey

At Jogbra, we were interested in and committed to growth—and I don't only mean in terms of the business. Growth as it pertained to the business was just a fact of life that had to be dealt with, like puberty. Growth was the nature of this entity that had been birthed, and we had to respond to it as best we could. We did not need to pursue it. We just needed to survive it.

The growth I am referring to is of the personal variety. As women, growing up in the 1950s, we were aware of the various and plentiful counterculture directives. There was a sense of felt responsibility to explore our options as human beings—to push perceived limits.

It is easy now, after years of experience and study, to throw down a few words and phrases to articulate the situation. But back in the first few years of Jogbra—a growing entity of people trying to work together while headed by two very different young women—we were swimming through murky water toward a sunny shore, but in the daily swimming, we had no idea if we were making any headway.

It could feel confusing. Scary. Lonely.

The "lonely" happened for me in great part because my business partner had chosen to treat me as an adversary, not a partner. So, although she was a strong swimmer, I felt alone in those new waters. Her attitude did not jibe with the yoga teacher, vegetarian woman I had brought into my business in 1977, and I became confused, saddened, angered, and even ashamed. Her behavior was an anathema to the "nice girl" directives of my childhood.

While painful, it was a tremendous lesson—one I am still, and almost always, in the throes of learning. It is a basic lesson, but one we often forget between classes. Unfortunately, not everyone respects the values and mores of others when they are different from our own. On this occasion my takeaway was a question: *What new skills and strengths are of use and can be found here, and do I even want to master all of them?*

A popular bumper sticker of the Vietnam era was "Challenge Authority." This resonated with my youthful self. As a business owner, though, I had become the "authority." When I walked through that office door each morning, I was the authority to a group of people and a mission that we had all contracted to fulfill. This was a new experience for me, something I needed to get my head around. What did it mean to have authority over others? How was I going to wield my authority?

Over the years, talking to many business owners, it has become abundantly clear to me that you cannot successfully grow a business if you are not willing to grow personally. We must grow *with* our businesses. During those Jogbra years, I had to learn to evolve beyond my hippie-dippie and rather simplistic idea of power—one in which I considered it only a blunt tool for those interested in oppression and repression. No, I came to understand that being powerful was not bad and that power need not be a force for oppression. It sounds so basic now, but between the culture of the times and my upbringing, it took me a while to stop giving my power away, thinking of power only as an ugly, unattractive attribute. It took me too long, really, to realize that it is not having power that is the issue, but how we use our power that matters.

The question of power and the responsibility that comes with power is a timely one now. No matter what its scale—parent or president, boardroom or bedroom—any exercise of power leads to a choice: Power *over* or power *with*? Is one creating competition or collaboration? This is relevant to consider especially now, as we move toward deeper understandings of how our universe works. On all fronts, we are less and less operating in an "either/or" paradigm. In fact, it is my observation that this polarizing era has really passed, and that of "both/and" is settling firmly into our collective psyches.

I am reminded of something I heard Marianne Williamson say some years ago that caught my attention: "It is not our darkness that frightens us, but our light." Recently, I heard her repeat this sentiment a bit differently, saying, "It is the responsibility of our light, power, talent, abilities that amazes and can overwhelm us."

I am learning—and keep learning—to cultivate my strengths, wield my power with care, manage with compassion those who would have power over and oppress, and all the while cope with my overwhelm as it, inevitably, rises.

16.
A DAY IN THE LIFE

"Life shrinks or expands in proportion to one's courage."
~ Anais Nin

Someone asked me recently what my typical day was like when I was CEO of Jogbra Sports Bras. I had to laugh, because in my effort to answer this seemingly easy-breezy, softball question, I realized there was no such thing as a typical day.

It's actually a fantasy to think of oneself as the "boss" of any entrepreneurial endeavor. Rather, the company becomes the boss o' you! Once you commit to birthing "your baby," staying the course means doing what is needed to survive, grow, and remain healthy.

Throughout my tenure at Jogbra—whether my job title was President, CEO, Co-President, Founder, or Co-Founder—I felt the title didn't really mean anything, except perhaps to the outside world. My day-to-day job was to get products made, marketed, and sold. The tasks I actually performed on a day-to-day basis ranged from the very simple and immediate to the very complex and visionary. The old chestnut is true: you wear a lot of hats when you're an entrepreneur.

In the early months and first year of the business, my Katharine Gibbs secretarial training and experience in different secretarial stints came in handy. I had worked in various sectors—social services and education, as well as in private, for-profit enterprises and corporations. I knew we needed filing systems—yes, plural—and I knew how to set them up. I just didn't want to have to maintain them. So, besides the necessary packing and shipping clerk, two early hires were an administrative assistant (read Jill o' All Trades) and a bookkeeper. For immediate outside help, I knew we needed legal, accounting, advertising, and marketing support.

A "typical day" in the start-up phase of Jogbra focused on finding and enrolling those who could help create and establish the Jogbra Sports Bras organization. We needed to create the type of relationships that would support and nurture our business. After that, I might say that a typical day was spent responding to the consequences of those engagements! As far as the legal and accounting area, aside from the patent process, so much of it was necessary but mind-numbing minutiae.

And here is another aspect of a typical day for any woman in business in the 1970s and 1980s: our silence. These days—how many years later?—people like Pat

Mitchell (TEDWomen, past President & CEO of PBS) are speaking up about the silence of women regarding sexual harassment, condescension, and lack of ability of women to support one another in the workplace. And somehow, I had missed the class about competing with other women in the workplace. Perhaps because I'd never developed that sort of ambition? At any rate, I had come onto the scene naïvely holding a "sisterhood" belief that we were all allies in the face of the patriarchy. I only wrote out my confusion and pain in my journals, or it would show up in my doodles and flow out through my art.

There was a great deal to do in the early days of Jogbra. So much depended upon the acceptance of our product in the marketplace. We were, quite literally, moving from nonexistence into existence. For this, we needed advertising and marketing. We needed to let "the world" know about Jogbra—not only our customers, but the stores that we needed to carry our product. This was no small task in the pre-internet, pre-social-media decades. Luckily, I actually had a knack for this part of the business. It was the creative, communicative realm of Jogbra.

I understood the importance of marketing, perhaps because of my father, or perhaps because my studies (and inherent interests) were in education. And, as I quickly grasped, introducing a new product concept into an industry was all about educating the dealers, the sales representatives that called on those dealers, and the customers.

We needed to capitalize on the media attention we were receiving. It was a good story: how two jockstraps were cut up and sewn back together to become a new kind of bra for athletic women. And beneath the cuteness of the story was the rapidly dawning reality that women did indeed have a need for their own "athletic supporter."

Those early years were all about travel. If it wasn't a rep wanting me to go with him or her on a sales call to an important account, it was a request to attend a regional show or race event. I went to every region of the country during those first few years and I met a lot of people.

My "typical day" would also include a lot of time on the telephone encouraging and guiding our sales representatives, who were scattered all over the country. As the number of reps grew, I realized that my by-the-pants, learn-as-I-go method of managing sales was not going to be adequate. I knew we needed a "real" sales manager, one whose profession, by choice, was truly sales. I needed someone who had studied sales and had a successful track record.

All this time, I had also been creating the annual sales forecast. It was a natural extension of those "Financial Fairy Tales" I'd created for the SBA loan in the very beginning of our journey. Only now, it was based on actual numbers. Each year's projection was based on the previous year's history—finally, something real! I would hole up at home with all the files and sales histories spread around me on my dining-room table and project our sales—by style (when we started having more than one), by month—for the upcoming year. These quantities would then translate into both our projected revenues as well as inform our production schedule. My next task in this process was to turn to the sales territories and allocate sales goals to each rep group. *Voila!* We had a sales plan.

Well, we always had a plan to *start* with. But as the actual numbers would start rolling in, we would have to adjust and then compare our "plan to actuals." It was always exciting—how'd we do? This was the crux of the game: create a goal and then try to achieve it. Put a team together to help you play. Then, go out and play! Or—as more serious business types might say, "Plan your work then work your plan."

The sales projection was our base plan; it structured the rest of our game plan. Once formed, I would communicate it to the sales rep organizations. On her end, Hinda and the production team would translate these sales projections into future production levels. Then, these would get communicated to both our raw inventory vendors and the factory. As the plan morphed and changed, we all had to be flexible and responsive.

In the midst of all the busyness, travel, and activity, I created a simple, but very important, guideline for myself—one that I had to pay attention to every morning no matter where I was. During that first thirty- to forty-five-minute period after waking, I had to run an interior "systems check." Was I experiencing any seizure activity? I had come to know my pattern. If I was going to have epileptic activity, it was typically in the mornings upon waking. That is when my ghostly "partner" would show up. I was blessed in this way, really. It was the predictable aspect of a very unpredictable element in my life, and such timing had its advantages. There were, inevitably, occasions when I missed the signs or denied them because I needed or wanted to get to a meeting, catch a plane, or show up for whatever—but those instances were not the norm. On my "typical day," I would wake up, putter about getting coffee or doing other relatively safe morning activities before getting in the shower and driving to work. Most Jogbra employees knew not to schedule early morning meetings with me, unless I *had* to be in attendance. Not everyone always remembered, but they tried.

Every day was an adventure. As I've said, it's difficult to outline a "typical day." When talking about the phenomenon of starting and running the Jogbra organization, it might be more correct to speak of its phases—start-up, growing, and then maybe (at least for me) the last phase would be *leaving*. How we operated in each phase had different needs and required different skills.

The other routine I tried to make time for in my increasingly hectic schedule was running. My runs were getting shorter, though. Jogbra was taking a lot out of me. Even getting out at lunchtime had become difficult. I wasn't running as much as I had before. But the apartment I moved into after leaving College Street, on Colchester Avenue, presented fresh running routes and challenges. It was on a busier street and steeper hill—but you couldn't be a runner in Burlington and not confront hills of one degree or another. Luckily, the area behind me was flatter and less busy. If I waited to get home before taking a run, I could go out Patchen Road, which in those days still had a lot of woods, a park, and even a riding stable. Otherwise, I would try to take a run right out of the offices on Clarke Street, where my old routes were still easily accessible. From there, I'd head up Loomis Street to Mansfield Avenue and over through the UVM campus into familiar territory. I treasured my time running and being out in nature. It rejuvenated me.

Thump, thump, thump.

The sound of my feet hitting the soft, leaf-damp ground as I ran through the autumnal Red Rocks Park in Burlington on the shore of Lake Champlain. The trees had shed some of their leaves, but there would be more to fall. Red and orange maple bits mingled with the brown and green under my running shoes—the smell of earth and leaves was rich in my nose. I could see my breath on this October afternoon and felt my heart pounding in sync with my feet.

"Listen, listen, listen to my heart's song," I sang softly to myself, as I moved along the path. "Listen, listen, listen to my heart's song. I will never forget you. I will never forsake you. Listen, listen, listen . . ."

The path turned again, the trees opened up, and the vast lake revealed herself to me. The pale sun hung shrouded in clouds above the distant Adirondacks that slashed darkly between lake and sky. I ran along the edge, recalling the past summer, when my running partner and I would stop here, clamber down the big rocks, strip off shirts and shoes, and dive into the water to cool off. We'd just dip in, climb out, and dry off a bit in the sun before putting our shoes and shirts back on to continue our run. What joy!

Today, alone, with perspiration quickly chilling on my neck, I ran by this spot and then turned back into the silent trees toward my car on the edge of the park. My knee was bothering me again, and I had to return to work.

It was during this period that I first started noticing the pain. My left knee first, then shortly after my right knee began to throb. I'd taken to breaking up my runs with periods of walking. And no amount of stretching before or after my runs seemed to make a difference. Then, one day—maybe in mid-1980—I was going up some stairs and my left knee gave out altogether. I fell onto the step.

It was time to go see a doctor and find out what the heck was the matter.

17.

1 MILL STREET

"Confront the dark parts of yourself, and work to banish them with illumination and forgiveness. Your willingness to wrestle with your demons will cause your angels to sing."
~ August Wilson

As the 1980s dawned, my baby boomer generation was morphing yet again. We went from the laid-back 1970s to the "Gravy '80s" of the "Me generation" and Wall Street. From communes to condos, yoga studios to yachts, we were moving—perhaps unknowingly—from transformative to transactional.

It would prove to be a truly linchpin decade, starting off on a sad and ominous note when John Lennon was shot outside his New York City apartment building. Diana married Prince Charles in 1981, the AIDS epidemic began its global killing spree, and Nancy Reagan was telling us to "Just Say No." Sally Ride was the first woman in space in 1983, then in 1986 the Challenger blew up. That same year, the nuclear meltdown in Chernobyl scared the hell out of me. The stock market was booming, President Reagan was telling us about the "trickle-down economy," and we women were determined to have it all. Our mothers and older sisters had been confined to nursing, secretarial, and teaching jobs—their success defined by the socioeconomic status of the man they'd married, the squareness of his chin, and the all-American good looks of their children. But not us! We'd have our lovers, grab a husband (maybe), and never miss a beat climbing the success ladder of our chosen profession. Oh, and we'd have a few children along the way as well, if *we* chose.

And there were examples showing how that out-of-the-box thinking was beginning to find mainstream acceptance and popularity. The movie *E.T.* was released and attracted huge and varied audiences, Geraldine Ferraro became the first woman ever to run as a vice presidential nominee (with Walter Mondale), and Michael Jackson released "Thriller." By 1984, Madonna was dancing on the stage, singing "Like a Virgin" in what looked like only a bra. In 1985, Live Aid erupted on everyone's television sets and Queen sang "We Are the Champions," rocking out almost the entire globe. Indicators, all.

Disco was still king in the music and club world, but I didn't know much about that—music on my radio was Springsteen's newly released *Born in the USA*, U2's *Joshua Tree*, and Windham Hill's instrumental anything. Sitting in a bar in Burlington while waiting for a business associate,

I first heard Pachelbel's "Canon in D" and fell in love with it, beginning what was to become a lifelong, if unschooled, love of classical music.

On TV, *The Oprah Winfrey Show* first appeared in 1986—casting a truly different and refreshingly honest image and attitude across our feminine psyches. I cried when *M*A*S*H* ended in 1983, but by 1987 had fallen in love with the new *Star Trek*, in spite of the weird guy over-playing Captain Kirk—wasn't it William somebody?

At the start of the decade, I didn't even own a television set. Al had taken our old TV when he moved out of College Street, and I had never replaced it. But when 1980 rolled in, bringing with it the Winter Olympics in Lake Placid, New York, I had to rethink my situation. I had to have a TV to watch the Olympics, or so I told myself. It was related to my business, was my argument. And Lake Placid was right in our backyard, I rationalized. I *needed* a TV.

We saw the Olympics that year as an opportunity for Jogbra. Somehow their close geographical proximity made it seem less outrageous for us to approach the Olympic Committee with our bid for a sponsorship. Hinda and I took an airplane ride over Lake Champlain to get to Lake Placid. I don't know why we thought to do this—it was only a couple of hours away by car. It was a small prop plane and an uncomfortable, bumpy ride. I am used to flying, but this was not a fun trip, but we made it. And in that meeting we somehow finagled the right to put the

Olympic sponsorship logo on our bras' packaging! When I think of it now, I don't know how we justified it—there is no running in the Winter Olympics. And we had no money. But somehow, we earned the right to put an Olympic seal on our packaging and in our very first ad that year. Pesky women! Brilliant women!

By 1980, we were already outgrowing our Clarke Street offices. At some point that year Hinda moved back to New York City and was operating out of an apartment she'd found on the Upper West Side. I have forgotten all the reasons she gave me for this move, but I was not going to stand in her way. Frankly, it was a relief. She made a case for how it would help our company to have a presence in New York, where the fabric suppliers were based, where Mel had an office, and where we could have meetings, etc.

I think Hinda was disenchanted with Burlington at that time. I remember her frequent complaints in those early years about living there. I supposed it was a big change from Montreal, where she'd grown up, and Manhattan, where she'd gone to school. It made an impression on me when, one Monday morning, she came into the office asking if I still had a copy of yesterday's Sunday *New York Times*. When I replied that I did—it usually took me a few days to get through it—she said she needed to have it when I was done as she had not been able to get a copy the day before. She then went on a rant about how Burlington completely closed down on Sundays, how one could not buy chocolate and a Sunday newspaper in the same place, and on and on. I thought the degree of her upset seemed a bit more than the disappointment called for, but I listened.

It was the first time I considered that perhaps she was unhappier than I had realized and that the anger I felt from her was in part fueled by that unhappiness. So when she made a case for how it would help Jogbra to have a presence in New York, I did not argue. I did not buy it, but I didn't argue. At that point, her move was good for both of us.

Besides, I was trying to deal with my own demons. A few months before, I had moved into a new apartment and had a very bad convulsion there. Being new in the space, I had not yet "trained" myself about safe falling spaces and places. As a result, I had cracked my head open on the sharp edge of a heavy butcher-block table in the tiny galley kitchen. Head wounds bleed a lot so when I came to, I found myself surrounded by blood everywhere. I mean *everywhere*—the linoleum tile floor was covered.

The head injury was par for the course of what was, for me, a very bad year—divorce finalizing, moving, my cat dying, my father dying, and then having this very bad convulsion and head injury, which negatively impacted my health for at least the next six months.

Perhaps as a result of my increased seizure activity, the neurologist added another anticonvulsant to my medication regime. I didn't know to protest, so I started taking it and life went on. But almost immediately, I started to feel poorly. I began spiraling downward—feeling sad, heading into depression. My thinking was foggy. My body was sluggish. I don't think other people noticed, but I did. My quick repartee was gone. Words, in general, did not come easily. As the months rolled on, the fog became thicker.

At first, I attributed these changes to the pressures of the business. My running routine was also off—another contributor to that year from hell. My left knee had blown out and my right knee continued to bother me, so I was having a really hard time running. Sometimes I couldn't run at all. Not having my regular running routine made me grouchy and fed the depression. But my intuition told me it was more than not getting in my run and more than entrepreneurial stress. Something bigger was going on—the brain fogginess I was experiencing was too weird. (One of the silver linings of having a chronic medical condition is that you learn to pay attention, to take your body's signals seriously.)

I took myself to a doctor. Eventually—not immediately, not quickly—he uncovered the cause of my inner grayness. It was a simple blood test that revealed the answer. The second epilepsy drug, Mysoline, was interacting with the first one I'd been prescribed, and it was turning into a *barbiturate* in my bloodstream. In essence, it was creating a drug cocktail in my system. Over time, it was building up in my body, progressively drugging me. I had not been wrong—my brain fogginess had been getting thicker.

Although the doctor counseled a slow withdrawal, I went home and immediately stopped taking what to me was "the evil drug." I promptly had another massive, awful grand mal convulsion. You can't just do that. So, as originally advised, I had to go back on the drug and slowly reduce the amount I was taking. The good news was I carried on and the damn fog began to lift. But it took years to get off the Mysoline entirely, and then to actually get it out of my system completely. Throughout this medication mess, I continued to go to work every day—talking to bankers, sales reps, staff, and Hinda, who was now working from her apartment in Manhattan and coming up to Vermont as needed.

Through it all, Jogbra just kept growing.

While Hinda's move to NYC relieved some of the space congestion we were experiencing in the office, we desperately needed real warehouse and shipping space. Finding us new digs went onto my to-do list.

In an old, three-story, brick woolen mill I found our ideal space. Winooski was once a thriving mill town, and those mills bracketed the Winooski Falls on either side of a bridge that connected the town with its historically more prosperous sister—and Vermont's largest town—Burlington. The mill I was eyeing, 1 Mill Street, was built in 1912 and overlooked the Winooski River falls. It had been long abandoned and empty for decades until early in the 1980s, when an enterprising developer rehabbed it and reinvented it as an "incubator space." It was ideal for artists and start-ups. The vast top floor of "The Chace Mill" became the Jogbra Sports Bras new headquarters and warehouse space. And, boy oh boy, did we now have warehouse and shipping space—and room to expand when we needed it. We had arrived.

It was fun to oversee the remodel of this fabulous old space. It was a blank canvas. I learned to deal with contractors, navigate the permitting process, and move through the ins and outs of "leaseholder improvements" in general.

Originally, the space was wide open; I believe it was used for sewing machine lines or some sort of other machine operations. (Ironic, eh?) The wide, wooden-planked floors, a warm orangey brown, were stained with a deeper, dark chocolate in spots where machine oil once dripped. On its front side, there were big windows facing the bridged, ever-moving river. I put my office here, as well as one for Hinda. A large open area housed our receptionist, and a row of offices was built along the western wall. Because all the ceilings were very high, some of the offices didn't really have ceilings. Rather, they were just walled enclosures. This was far, far before the "open space" and cubicles concepts had become popular. But I wasn't a believer in cubicles, anyway. No, I built enclosed offices, ceilings or no. Of course, we agreed to have a shower installed in the bathroom for the runners among us. Unfortunately, I would be using it less and less with time, as my knees were really slowing me down. Going up and down the three flights of stairs to our new offices was challenge enough.

Every doctor I visited told me the same thing: stop running. I was so sad. In fact, I was depressed. Now, studies show that those who have to stop their regular exercise regime routinely spiral into depression. At the time, though, we didn't know about endorphins, and I didn't know what had hit me. I was blaming it all on the effects of the debacle with my medications. I knew I missed running. I knew it was an important outlet for the daily tensions of being an entrepreneur. But I was unprepared for what was happening to me. And I was gaining weight, which caused me to become even more upset. It was during this period that I began to feel rather like a fraud—the Jogbra inventor who can't run *and* is out of shape and overweight. Whether real or imagined, I felt that people were judging me. *I* judged me.

Just before moving into our new offices, I finally hired a National Sales Manager. It was time to have a sales "professional" handling the reps and our sales plan, instead of me. We found Frank Nevins, an ambitious young man who helped the company transition the position and helped me move away from my day-to-day dealings with the accounts and the reps. He was good for us, but Jogbra was just a stepping-stone for him. When Frank moved on, we really hit our stride when we brought Jan Kimbrell in-house.

Jan had done an excellent job as our independent sales rep for Southern California, teaching me a great deal along the way. We'd become friends. I am wont to make friends with those I work with—it is only logical to me, really. There are so many shared experiences, concerns, and goals. It is difficult to not be friends, unless there is an egregious breach of trust. So, when Jan expressed an interest in coming in-house, in essence leaving her own business to become a part of mine, I was both surprised and delighted. There was no question in my mind about her qualifications or ability. When she flew out for the official interview, most of my questions were about this big life change for her: leaving her business, moving from Southern California to Vermont, no longer being "independent" but salaried instead. All of these were big changes and things that I, as the potential employer, had to consider. We were growing so quickly. Jan would be the third person (counting me) in this position. I wanted and needed it to stick.

It stuck. Bringing Jan in was one of the best decisions I made at Jogbra. She was the sales professional with the experience and depth of knowledge that we needed. And it is important to note, I think, that Jan and I did not always agree. We had different work styles, and she could drive me crazy. I'm sure I drove her crazy, too. She might leave things right up to the last minute, which would press all my "worry buttons." But in the end, she always got the job done. She met virtually every sales goal and plan, often exceeding them. So as frustrated or worried as I might have been along the way, I had to admit that her outcomes were stellar. Though our work styles were different, our values were the same. I came to understand this. Through Jan and many of our other employees, I was learning to trust that my way was not the only effective way. You'd think it would be an obvious lesson, but it was a hard one for me sometimes. I knew I had to master it, as it was so important for empowering our growing team.

18.

HEROINES

"Above all, be the heroine of your life, not the victim."
~ Nora Ephron

Sometime after we had settled into the Mill Street offices, Hinda returned to Vermont. She had nowhere to live, so for a time she chose to live in her "new" office. Suddenly, there was a mattress on the floor and clothing draped on her office furniture. This was a bit uncomfortable for some of our employees as our offices were not terribly soundproof and she was living there with her then boyfriend. Some mornings, one or both would troop across the open office space in a bathrobe to go to the bathroom to shower. Unfortunately, it would not always be before our rather prim and shy receptionist got to her desk in the morning. When I mentioned to Hinda that the situation was making some employees uncomfortable, she became annoyed, saying, "That's their problem!"

In truth, I did not begrudge her staying in her office while looking for a more permanent living arrangement.

After all, we started with those hippie-dippie ideals. Unconventional was part of how we stayed on the creative, entrepreneurial curve. If my conventional, good-girl self raised an eyebrow, my artist self quickly swatted it down. Hinda was in transition. This was her office. It was a perk of being the boss. What both of my selves did feel was that she went too far by inviting someone else to stay in her office with her. It felt a line had been crossed.

Eventually, of course, Hinda found an apartment and moved out of the office, to a few sighs of relief. But with Hinda's reappearance, the tension in our office returned. The tension between us was always visible—and audible— and *everyone* felt it.

On the one hand, while both Hinda and I were interested in our own personal growth, our interaction in the office was civil at its best and disgraceful at its worst. Perhaps this was distressing to me because the fundamental relationships of my childhood were troubled, far from idyllic. My parents fought often, my father yelling loudly and nastily at my mother, my mother stoically not responding or murmuring snide asides when he was out of earshot.

So when Hinda routinely yelled at me in the office during those first four years, I would be triggered and withdraw or respond with snarky sarcasm—sometimes both. Too many of our discussions devolved into arguments, turning the energy in the room darkly electric.

Our employees were victims of this tension. It wasn't pretty. It embarrassed me, even then. It was the very opposite of what I believed an enlightened, compassionate, and collaborative partnership should look like—and most definitely the opposite of what I had envisioned when Polly, Hinda, and I started out in my living room at 359 College Street. This relationship was the very opposite of the counterculture values we had both professed to embrace: love, cooperation, peace. But then Hinda would offer yoga classes to everyone, out in the hallway at 1 Mill Street. Or we might agree to have a staff training, bringing in a coach or personnel expert or some such to do something that benefitted everyone. We were rather like parents trying to make up for bad behavior.

I was ashamed of my dysfunctional relationship with Hinda and of her apparent negative feelings toward me. Raised to be a "lady," in those long-ago 1950s, we were supposed to be, above all, proper, liked, accepted. Appearances mattered. It was, I realized later, why I had stayed in my marriage for so long—my husband and I had appeared to others to be just fine! And while I understood clearly the inherent superficiality of this directive—not to mention the resultant oppression of many a woman—to be on the receiving end of so much undisguised, negative judgment was a brutal, scab-ripping way to confront my conditioning. And not just about the expectations my upbringing had embedded, but also about my more current cultural ones, the values and expectations I had taken on and chosen as a young woman. This negativity was at the hands of a woman! So my belief in and need for the "sisterhood" mythos—women for women and all that—was being battered. Oh man, I was struggling.

As a result, I mostly "kept up appearances" to the outer world—much as I had done in my marriage. Only my close friends knew of the pain and discomfort I was experiencing on the job. Even then, however, I don't think many I told took it seriously. I was my own boss, wasn't I? Running my own company? Besides, my adversary was a woman. How could I complain? How bad could it be? Even my own sister said, "It's not like you've been physically assaulted or anything. It doesn't compare!"

Here's the thing: on a deep level, I concurred. I was responsible for my own situation. I was complicit in this arrangement. And so, I felt shame. I also looked for answers: How had I been complicit in creating this?

There are a number of incidents that crystallized the impasse that Hinda and I faced as businesspeople and as humans. I remember one day Hinda was standing in the door of my office, and we were discussing something and, per usual, not seeing eye to eye. I wish I could recall exactly what the topic of our discussion was, but I don't. What I do remember is saying something along the lines of, "That scares me," or "It is a scary plan." The words were barely out of my mouth when Hinda interrupted, launched into my office, thrust her face into mine, and yelled, "Don't use that word! Scared! What is there to be frightened of? I hate that word!" She went on, loudly and angrily deriding me about being scared, afraid, timid.

Under my immediate response to her—of anger, defensiveness—I realized that her words really took me aback. No one had ever called me out about my anxiety and fear before. I was embarrassed. I was a "fraidy-cat" and she had called me out.

After she'd left, however, something else about the exchange lingered with me. Something else was going on with her, I knew—but what? I had this nagging feeling for a while, and then I put my finger on it: I recognized fear in *her*. She had reacted so vehemently, I believed, because my fear had triggered her own insecurities, and she couldn't have it. Like knows like. We were *both* struggling with the constant anxiety and stress of dealing with the unknowns of an expanding business. It was a major *aha!* moment for me. We were both young women in changing times—our own and that of the culture in which we were swimming.

I was no stranger to uncertainty and fear. Epilepsy had been a good teacher on that front. My constant relationship with the unknown and unpredictable made it easier for me to give my fears a voice. I think Hinda found that a sign of weakness. And perhaps in some instances, when I allowed the fear to cripple me, it was. She, on the other hand, felt she had to keep up a strong, invincible front, even to herself. In part, this was probably in response to the fear she read in me. She literally couldn't deal with any sign of "scared" in or from me, as it risked feeding and mirroring her own fears. Until that moment I hadn't understood this about her.

The teaching for me from that moment was strong and twofold. First, it reminded me to see beyond the book's cover. Clearly, I had not been "seeing" beyond Hinda's brash and brave front. Second, it taught me not to be so fast to reveal my own fears to others, especially Hinda. I needed to take a page from my partner's playbook and make a brave show, even when I wasn't feeling it. As Hinda would say, "Fake it 'til you make it." It was one of her favorite sayings, which, until that moment, I had always privately disliked. Now, I was going to practice it.

As mentioned, when I formed the corporation in 1977, I also had to designate officers. I made myself president, Hinda vice president, and Polly secretary and treasurer. But now it was 1981, and the day had come when Hinda wanted this to change. I believe we had just moved into our Mill Street offices when Hinda approached me about our titles. She let me know that she felt being *vice* president did not accurately reflect her position in the company to the outside world. She wanted to be president.

Sometimes she could really take me by surprise. When I responded that president was my position, my title, she spun out a rationale about how "vice" wasn't appropriate given the situation. In order for others to take her seriously, Hinda said she needed to have the president moniker.

I was sitting there, opposite her, taking it all in. Inspired, I asked her if she wouldn't rather be chief executive officer. That position was, after all, superior to the president—or so I said. I thought so, but I didn't really know. Hinda responded, "No." She wanted to be president. She wanted my title.

It was within my power to deny her. Power—that word, that concept, that *game*. I did not like being put in this position. I knew it was a lose-lose proposition for me. If I denied Hinda's request, I felt I would implicitly be buying into the notion of a power hierarchy. Not to mention, I would have to deal with Hinda's response to my denial. And why? Because of my own ego and its considerations on the matter? Oh, I really did not like being put in this position.

So I laughed and said, "Okay. Sure, Hinda, you can be president and I will be the CEO." And that was that. Did that make me a coward or a saint? Neither. It just made me a survivor and a seeker still seeking—perhaps one who was still afraid of the responsibility of her own power.

I don't know why Hinda felt the need to raise her voice to me in the office. It certainly wasn't an effective way to work with me. And whenever a disagreement about something carried on beyond one or two discussions, she would pull out the "I'm the majority shareholder, do as I say" card. After our first year or so, I realized that the "yogi woman" persona I had first encountered in Hinda was not going to reappear—that *that* had probably been the anomaly. I suspected that she was simply trying to force me out of the business. So, my inherent stubbornness kicked in. No way. A competitive part of me came to the fore. No way!

Honestly, I had never thought of myself as competitive until I found myself embroiled in this whole Jogbra battle, a world I had cocreated. Not only was there the usual competition with other brands and the outside world, which comes with any business. But there was this unwanted competition and power struggle with Hinda and how I was handling that. I had to ask myself: How much of our tension was rising out of ego? And not the good kind. I shuddered to think. But deep down, I knew that Hinda (like epilepsy) was another of my shadow teachers.

This was the undercurrent as the products flourished and the business continued to grow. But the resultant constant engagement in what felt like a relentless battle with my business partner was taking its toll. In the push-pull of my endeavor to not only hold on to my business but also stay both emotionally and physically healthy, I was losing that part of the battle. I'd gained a significant amount of weight, a direct result of no longer being able to run. Eating replaced running as my way to deal with the stress. And I had even started smoking cigarettes, sneaking them. What, I wondered, had happened to that strong, confident young runner who'd had the courage to strike out on her own, start graduate school and a business, and face living alone?

And finally, as 1982 dawned, I had had enough.

It was time to give in, to surrender. If my business partner wanted me out, as so many of her actions had indicated over the past four-plus years—fine, I'd go. I needed to unleash myself from this whole crazy situation. I needed to take care of myself. But what I needed to do in order to manifest this was difficult for me. It had taken me four years to make the decision to take my next action.

That spring, I wrote Hinda a letter telling her that either I would buy her out (which I knew was doubtful), or she must buy me out, or we must equalize the shares. I would no longer endure our partnership dynamics as they had evolved based on the unequal distribution of shares. I put the letter in her inbox and then got on a plane and went on vacation to Guadeloupe—with Polly, by the way.

Hinda was furious. Upon my return, she yelled at me for giving her an ultimatum and then leaving. But she was going to buy me out, she declared. She had spoken with her father and she would buy my shares. We hired the lawyers to draw up an agreement. Over the next month or so, we proceeded to spend thousands of dollars on legal fees to craft the buyout agreement. In my head, I was packing my bags. In real time, I was perusing photos of real estate in Hawaii. I was outta Vermont.

One afternoon, I was sitting at my desk—the same big, old, oak desk—when Hinda came reeling into my office. "I've been out riding my bike and thinking," she declared as she plunked down in the chair opposite my desk.

"About what?"

"About something my father said to me about running this business. In our discussions about Jogbra's future, he told me that I probably couldn't run it by myself—that I'd need to find another partner. He asked me, did I want the headache I knew or a new headache I didn't know? That's what I've been thinking about."

I just sat there looking at her. Probably, I was glowering. "So?" I said. She wasn't looking at me, but out the window at the late spring sun.

"Soooooo. Maybe I will . . . I mean, I *will* sell you enough shares back to equalize ownership—at their current value, of course!" She turned back to me to emphasize that last phrase. "We'll become equal partners. The headache I *know*, you see."

I could not believe what I was hearing. *Now* she was willing to equalize the shares, after all these hours and dollars with the lawyers to craft a buyout? After I had done my emotional leave-taking from my baby? After bullying me for all these years? Because I'm the preferable headache? Without conscious volition, my arm rose up over my head and my fist slammed down on my desk. We both jumped.

"I'll think about it!" I said through clenched teeth. But she wasn't done.

"Oh, and you have to get those last twenty shares Polly still has. Buy those from her too, at the same time, so it's just you and me. Nobody with a swing vote ability!"

This last requirement of Hinda's offer hit hard. How could I do that? I felt badly enough about allowing Polly's critical early contributions to be glossed over during the past four years of Jogbra's history. I cringed every time I heard the credit for her work going elsewhere . . . and now this? Take away Polly's chance of participating in any final payoff this business might have in the future? Again, I hated being in this position. I felt like some character right out of a Greek tragedy, my foe pitting me against my childhood friend to resolve a long-standing issue.

This business was *my* creation. I had made friends in the course of building and running it. So much of the work that had been done was not only about Jogbra, but me. I had grown and prospered, overcome a lot of my perceived obstacles, and was conquering more all the time. As difficult as my partnership with Hinda was, it was forcing me to confront my fears and move out of my comfort zones. Plural. Also, to sell to Hinda would feel like defeat. She had been trying to force me out ever since she bought eighty of the one hundred shares I had issued to Polly all those years earlier. My competitive streak really did not want to concede to Hinda, the headache I knew.

With a heavy heart, I agreed. I called and spoke to Polly. I flew down to New York where she was living and, with difficulty and through tears, she agreed to sell me her remaining shares in order to help end this mess with Hinda. It was one of the most difficult conversations I have ever had to have. My dear friend's willingness to do this for me renewed my faith in the concept of "sisterhood" to a significant degree. It does exist, it is just not universal, and it does not come automatically with the genitalia.

I returned to Vermont and stated my conditions: I would agree to purchase Hinda's excess shares at their then current value—value which I, of course, had helped to create, but now had to pay for. I would sign a note, payable only when we realized the worth of those shares—most likely, we both understood, at the sale of the business. Also, I instructed Hinda that we must form an advisory board of directors that we would turn to for counsel when we could not agree. I was determined to stop our ugly fights.

Hinda consented.

And so, four years after first revealing to me that she had bought Polly's shares and intended to be boss-lady-majority-shareholder, finally we were once again equal partners in the business.

For quite a period of time after our equity positions were equalized, a semblance of civility returned to our interactions—not that we began to socialize with one another, except when professional circumstance dictated it. We didn't. Still, our relationship had reached a new plateau. Although we only poorly articulated it at the time, we knew this: we were witnesses to the evolution of women in sports, and we were the stewards of a very special ingredient in that evolution—the sports bra.

Inside the office, by the mid-1980s, we were aware of and actively working on being conscious of what sort of culture we were creating at our company. In this new era of our "equalization," the tensions between Hinda and me diminished and were felt less by others. Thus, our attention and intentions were able to broaden.

Luckily, in the early '80s era of self-awareness and personal growth gurus, we found an organization called Human Factors. In our spiritual pursuits, both Hinda and I had gone to the Human Factors workshops. I'd been to several, and one we had even attended together.

While there were a lot of programs and "New Age" theorists out and about in those days, we found Human Factors to be trustworthy and, most importantly, useful. Developed by an organizational development guy, the late John Thompson, I found his use of then innovative psychological techniques in management training very helpful. The emphasis was on personal awareness, value clarification, and the development of a resultant congruent business culture. Just what the doctor ordered! It also echoed and validated my growing knowingness that I had to grow personally in order to keep up with, facilitate, and guide the Jogbra business's phenomenal growth.

John believed that doing personal work and introspection in a compressed and intense, weeklong program would be enhanced if done in beautiful and serene surroundings. This spoke to me; I knew it to be true. To this end, the first time I did his program was in Hawaii. Another time, in a pristine area of Georgia. And then, of course, beautiful Vermont.

One of the exercises in a Human Factors workshop was one in which two participants would sit opposite each other and one would ask the other, "Who are you?" Upon Participant 2's answer, Participant 1 would reply, "Thank you. Tell me who you are." This was done repeatedly, until the answering partner ran out of answers. It might go something like this.

Participant 1: "Tell me who you are."
Participant 2: "Sally."
Participant 1: "Thank you. Tell me who you are."
Participant 2: "A wife."
Participant 1: "Thank you. Tell me who you are."
Participant 2: "A sister."

This would go on as the responding partner ran through all the obvious answers (woman, sister, daughter, artist, nurse, bitch, gardener, boss. . .). The answers would get deeper and deeper, on into the more esoteric labels one might adopt, until finally beyond all labels and personae. Then the two people in the partnered positions would switch roles and begin again.

Participant 1: "Tell me who you are."
Participant 2: "Lisa."

Sound crazy? It was a powerful experience. Humbling. I learned, decades later while in graduate school, that this exercise was an adaptation of one done by young men training to become Buddhist monks.

Besides having programs for individual work, Human Factors also had corporate programs. Indeed, that is where John Thompson began. So, because we knew and trusted that group, we wanted to share some semblance of our experience with the entire company. We decided to bring them in-house for a 360 review—which, as you might imagine, was met with mixed enthusiasm at the time—but we did it anyway.

With a prescribed set of questions, all full-time employees got to review each other, no matter their position in the company. The exercise provided yet another important lesson: I learned there was a disparity between how I thought I came across as a "boss" and how I was in fact perceived by some in the company. *Hmmm*. Specifically, it was the observation that I could be distant and moody.

This feedback took me aback because having once been that girl out at the desk—a secretary, a filing clerk, low woman on the totem pole—I thought I was sensitive to most all the positions and people working at Jogbra. I'd been there, done that. I did not see myself as aloof or distant. I certainly didn't feel as if I acted in a snobbish manner, which is what I read into the comments. But I had to acknowledge the "moody" observation. I felt called out with that one. I knew I could be moody.

I reminded myself the comments were made by only some of the employees, not all. Yet, still they stung. It was a useful lesson, more fodder for my internal grist mill that was grinding away and sculpting the ever-evolving "Lisa"—no longer the "older, returning college student" or "epileptic" or "secretary." Even "the artist" had faded into the background. Coming forth and getting polished up now was Lisa the "entrepreneur," the *successful* entrepreneur, the "boss," the "independent woman." A Lisa who might recognize and befriend her own power.

And evidently she could be moody and didn't listen as well as she thought she did.

19.
WE HAD FUN

"When the working day is done, oh,
girls just wanna have fun!"
~ Cyndi Lauper

"**F**inding the funny" was one of my coping mechanisms for dealing with the stress of the earliest days of Jogbra's growth. Sometimes I found it in the irony or absurdity of my day. Other times it was just plain old silliness, manufactured and dished out at the end of a long day. As others came on board, this became easier, part of our culture.

By the mid-1980s, we were in a flow, still growing but managing our growth more efficiently, due in great part to our dedicated employees. Lydia, originally hired as our shipping clerk back at Clarke Street, had risen to warehouse manager and ran "out back" efficiently and smoothly. I'd hired a professional sales manager, and we had an actual customer service department with people on the phones to take orders. As our sales numbers climbed the organization had to grow to keep track of it all—in its number of people and its sophistication. As needed, we added positions to the finance and accounting department. Hinda had production assistants to help manage those assets. We also found Denni, our in-house designer, to help keep the product line fresh and to work with the factories.

My work style benefitted from a number of supportive helpers, organizers, and carry-outers. I am so appreciative of the women who helped me during those years. Judy, Mary Jane, Robin, Melissa, and Sue, to name a few. Each helped me in more ways than they may know. Not to mention the smiles and laughs each brought into my office. As the years passed, walking into the offices at 1 Mill Street had become like walking into my own little cosmos. The Jogbra company had become a busy, vibrant world.

My idea of fun had been hard to come by back in those very early '80s, when I was first traveling all over the country with our sales reps, people I did not yet know well and with whom I had to keep a professional rapport. That began to change when I hired and started working with first Jan Kimbrell and then, shortly thereafter, Norine Lassa. Of the many friends and colleagues I had met along the way outside of the office, these two stand out.

With both of these women, I was able to not only conduct productive and lucrative business, but we could also relax and have fun with one another. We might go out for dinner, go shopping, or dancing—or all three. Together, we would laugh about the day's events or nonevents, or just be silly. We shared a sense of humor and appreciation for one another. I met their friends and family and they met mine. We were kindred spirits, women of that changing time. We were trying to make a living, be our best selves, and somehow along the way find a guy to love and who could love us back—work, travel, ambitions notwithstanding. This turned out to be a tall order, but we did not know that then. We didn't even know we were still young or part of a wave of women in the same boat. In that time and place, we were just women doing our jobs, on a mission, and only dimly aware that it was not just one mission, but really many missions that were insidiously changing the socioeconomic and political landscape.

And I think it is worth noting, happily, that the three of us—Norine, Jan, and I—remain in touch to this day.

One of the things that I'd learned early on in my endeavor to "manage sales" was that we had to have something called a "national sales meeting" where we would bring all our sales representatives together in one place to get them revved up about our product and company—get them "on board" to meet their sales goals. We were still the little kid on the sporting goods block. How could we compete with the big sporting goods industry's approach to sales meetings? How could we capture the glitz and glamour that the shoe companies offered, for instance? Celebrity performances, abundant food, and flowing booze!

We found a way. Our sales meetings were fun. In having to compete with bigger companies, we got creative. We shaped a more personal, down-to-earth experience for our salespeople—one that lent itself not only to fun and camaraderie, but also to sharing and connection. We brought them to Vermont and had ski races, caricatures drawn, and fashion shows. Hinda, Jan, and I were accessible to our sales team, not just some people standing on a stage behind a microphone. Our customer service people were there as well, the people our reps spoke to on the phone all year long. It was important, I felt, to put faces to the voices. Relationships. It is all about relationships.

And we were a little crazy. One year I wrote a rap song, the "Jogbra Rap," which Hinda, Jan, and I actually performed at the event. We got a lot of laughs. Another time, our sales rep of the year was awarded a bronzed bra. Yes, an actual sports bra dipped in bronze and engraved with her name. Jealous?

Of course, there was the requisite info and training, which hopefully had the effect of incentivizing our sales reps and infusing them with our passion, so they could go out and sell more Jogbras. It worked, not with everyone and not all the time, but with many, with enough. Our staggering sales growth told the tale.

Soon after we had hit the market, all those standard, old bra manufacturers started coming out with their own version of a jogging bra. Due to our trademark, they could not call it a Jogbra, so they referred to their new products as "sports bras." *Ah, well,* I thought. *Imitation is the highest form of flattery!* These imitations were sold, of course, in their standard distribution channel—department store lingerie departments. But these early entries were, by and large, simply regular bras with different marketing and perhaps a different strap configuration, or some such. Our sales were not terribly impacted by these entrants. But we could not ignore that women shopped in those places. Once we were sophisticated enough (read Norine, Jan, and a good accounting department), it was time for us to play with those big boys.

We graduated from selling the Jogbra line of sports bras exclusively through small sporting goods stores and expanded, first, into the big sporting goods national chains and, second, into department stores. We had grown up enough to play in the big leagues. I don't think we could have done this without Jan and Norine's help. Most department stores had outlets all over the country with centralized buying offices, many of which were located in New York City—Norine's territory. As Norine prospered, she had taken on more lines, hired sub-reps, and landed and managed huge accounts. She was honest and considerate, and earned the trust of both manufacturers and buyers. She saw the opportunity, researched it, reviewed both the opportunity and the problems it presented, and worked out with us how Jogbra might start selling into department store lingerie departments without jeopardizing our position, image, and sales in the sporting goods market.

Our sales to large sporting goods chains of the day— like Herman's World of Sporting Goods, Big 5, Champs, and Sports Authority—had prepared us to enter the complex world of department store terms and conditions. It was no longer daunting. Also, by the mid-1980s, Jogbras and sports bras in general had become a highly accepted and desired item. Department stores wanted to stock them.

And so, the day came, with Norine's guidance, that we did begin selling to department stores, into their lingerie departments. We'd come full circle. Norine had a knack for making friends, and she had befriended the woman who was a buyer at Bloomingdale's. As a result, I ended up doing a personal-appearance tour at almost all the Bloomingdale's lingerie departments across the country— meeting and training the sales staff and meeting and greeting customers. ("Meet the inventor of the Jogbra! Today, 4–6 p.m., Bloomindale's lingerie department, third floor.")

I want to note here that Norine and Jan were reps carrying Jogbra together for many years before Jan moved in-house—first as National Sales Manager and then later as VP of Sales and Marketing. It says a great deal that their professional relationship not only weathered that transition but was strengthened by it. And that they are still friends to this day.

If it was true that, as our packaging stated for a while, "Lisa and Hinda—the brains behind the bras," it was Jan, Norine, and our other talented salespeople who were the company's strength and follow-through. Together they took Jogbra Sports Bras the distance. Without their help and support, we would not have been able to keep up with the demand we were experiencing.

And boy, were we experiencing demand! Jogbra was the right product at the right time. Women and girls were venturing forward—on the field and in life—experiencing the empowerment that being strong and athletic could provide. At Jogbra, we were both crafting and sharing that journey. It was an incredible run!

I think it was when we were at a Bloomingdale's in a suburb of Washington, DC that our fun brought one of us to a life-changing moment. It was springtime, the end of the day. After hours of standing under fluorescent lights in the Bloomingdale's lingerie department, Norine and I, wanting to be outside for a bit, went wandering through an interesting little shopping area. It was full of small cafes, galleries, artsy boutiques, and the like. We weren't the sort to head to a bar to unwind, and my running days were over by then. So, there we were, two colleagues, two young women, wandering down the springtime street, window-shopping. At one of the shops, I saw an outrageous pair of sunglasses. The frames were oversized around the eye area, looking to me very like hands with five fingers spread open, with the wearer's eyes being in the position of the palms. They were black plastic, with bright ruby-red, oval-shaped crystals at the end of each finger perfectly mimicking long fingernails. I had to have them.

We got back to our hotel around dinnertime and, tired, decided to just kick off our shoes, put on our pj's, and order in. But then, after plunking down on her bed, Norine looked at me and said, "This is crazy! Here we are, two single women in DC on a Friday night, and we are going to order room service? No! We should go out!"

"Of course. You are right," I said. "But I am too tired, really. All that standing and talking today—then walking. I'm a short hitter, I'm afraid!"

"Oh, come on, Lisa! It's DC! Let's go see what's going on out there! It'll be fun!" Norine urged. I could tell she was trying to convince herself as much as me. I didn't say anything in response; I hated clubs and the loud noise that passed for music in those days—we both did, really.

"I'm hungry. But let's not order in. Let's go down to the hotel's restaurant and then, after dinner, see how we feel."

That was our compromise—we would go downstairs for dinner. And the universe turned fate's wheel another notch.

"I'm going to wear my new sunglasses," I said as we headed out of our hotel room.

"Oh no! You can't!" Norine said, horrified, willing me back into the hotel room to put back my flashy new glasses.

"Yes, I am!" I said turning away and proceeding to the elevator. I pressed the down button and put on my crazy sunglasses.

"Oh, Lisa, what am I going to do with you? You take them off before we go into the restaurant, or I'm going to pretend I don't know you! I won't go in with you!" And laughing, we rode down the elevator.

The hotel restaurant wasn't very busy. As we approached the maître d', I kept on my sunglasses. With a big grin, I requested a table for two, though Norine was hanging back—*way* back. Well trained, the maître d' seated us without cracking a smile or a comment.

But the table next to us did.

There sat three attractive men, their finished dinner plates in front of them. They took one look at us, and the conversation began.

"Where did you get those bee-*yoo*-tiful sunglasses, may I ask?" one of them inquired.

"May we buy you both a drink?" another asked.

I could go into all the silly details of the ensuing evening. They were in town on business from the Midwest. We ate. They talked. We talked. We all flirted. There was a lot of laughter. They were nice guys. Music came on in the adjoining bar, and we all went in and danced together. It got late and I had to go to bed. Norine, however, had met Scott.

A year or so later, when they got engaged, I gave them those sunglasses as a silly engagement present. They sat on their fireplace mantel for years.

I have a photograph to remind me of another very fun night. It was a warm New York City night, made steamier by our laughter and silliness. Norine and I had just concluded business somewhere with some big account, perhaps seeing our buyer Becky at Bloomingdale's or calling on the buying offices of Foot Locker and Lady Foot Locker in the old Woolworth Building down on lower Broadway, which was a very cool old and historic building, the tallest in the world until 1930. Anyway, I don't remember exactly where we'd been earlier that day. What I do remember, with the help of this random photo, is that we still had the energy and will to have fun.

Norine's sister Ginny was with us. She was working with Norine by then, calling on accounts. We ended up in Little Italy, at Puglia's (still there the last time I was in the city). There were a lot of other people with us there as well, although for the life of me I can't recall who they were or how we knew them. Another rep group, maybe? Buyers? Friends? A mix of all of the above? It doesn't matter. We ate. We drank wine. We laughed. There was music, and we danced between the tables. At Puglia's, this was encouraged. It must have been a few weeks after our DC trip, as Scott had flown in from Wisconsin to spend time with Norine, surprising and impressing us both.

We were full of all that energy that comes from working long and hard, doing well, and knowing it. We had fun—such fun. The photo that keeps this memory alive for me is one of all of us at the table laughing and being silly. Ginny even had a parrot on her shoulder—yes, a parrot in a restaurant! What the picture does not fully reveal, and what I don't need it to help me remember, is what I felt like that evening. Happy, grown-up, and fulfilled. Being productive, working my "mission," and having fun with others who were working with me in that mission. It was a moment of balanced joy for me. And what made it really special is that I knew this in the moment.

20.

13 AVENUE D, WILLISTON

"The space within becomes the reality of the building."
~ Frank Lloyd Wright

I t was 1987, and we were doing very well. Both sales and profits were up. We had, in my opinion, a great team. Our organizational chart at that time had Hinda and me at the top and then our managers: Dave, Jan, Denni, Lydia, and Rosemary—finance, sales and marketing, design and production, warehouse and shipping, and human resources respectively. We met with these managers once a week on Thursday mornings.

Annually, Jan and I created the sales plan from which all else flowed. I developed the marketing and advertising strategy with Jan's info and expertise and Hinda's input. Denni and Hinda took care of the production plans, which at that point included the factories in Puerto Rico, Hong Kong, and China. We would review our plans regularly and adjust them as necessary—always leading to vibrant discussions! Because here is the elemental point: We all cared. *We. All. Cared.*

Jogbra had morphed from an idea, into a viable business, into a successful business, and then, finally, into a noticed player. We just didn't know yet all the levels of our significance—at least I didn't. But I believe many of us felt it.

Despite all the dysfunction between us, Hinda and I had somehow created a strong, vital culture. People cared about the Jogbra and how it was changing the landscape for athletic women. It may be a bit hyperbolic, but in those heady 1980s, I believe that for many of our employees, working for Jogbra was more than just a job. There was a sense of our shared vision and mission. I know that on occasion we discussed the fact that we were a bit . . . odd. It was not only that we were an anomaly as one of only two women-owned businesses in the sporting goods industry (Moving Comfort being the other, both of us 1977 start-ups). We sensed there was something more afoot.

There were so many—so *many*—people who helped and guided us, our "supporting cast" of characters. As I mentioned earlier, at one point we had a marketing ploy where little thumbnail headshots of Hinda and me appeared on all our packaging with the words "The Brains Behind the Bras" underlining our images. I always felt a bit squirmy about that phrase. It seemed misleading because we were so *not* doing this by ourselves, and really never had.

In-house we had what was overall a terrific and dedicated staff. We were very lucky. We did not have many difficult staffing issues over the years and were able to find talented and motivated people. In every area of the business—customer service, finance, admin and warehousing—it gives me more than a little satisfaction to know that some of the women at Jogbra were able to gain knowledge and experience that propelled them upward and forward. Meanwhile, out in the field were the buzzing and busy sales representatives and their organizations. It was amazing to have so many people out there carrying the Jogbra message and generating sales.

We had good support, too, from our advisory board first formed in late 1982, after Hinda and I equalized the shares. A word about the nature of our board: a privately held company such as ours could only have an advisory board, as Hinda and I were the only voting shareholders of our little corporation. We looked for and found people in the community who had experience and expertise in areas that we felt our business could benefit—finance, marketing, manufacturing, and such. And while my original intent was for the advisory board to help Hinda and me resolve some of our knottier disagreements, it never really came to that. This was due, at least in part, to the fact that the board's very existence provided us with a form of "exterior accountability"—a place to be heard and hear from others about whatever was going on in our business.

Just preparing for a board meeting was an excellent exercise in my own strategic-thinking process, and perhaps for Hinda's as well. It was no longer just the two of us that were at the envisioning, future, or planning level. The unhealthy dynamic that had developed—"my opinion versus yours"—was greatly ameliorated by having an objective sounding board, no pun intended. The group that we brought together provided input to our strategic-thinking and decision-making process. It helped to quell our communication difficulties. Whether preparing to educate or update our board members about our current status or present a specific problem for discussion, it elevated the discourse and depersonalized it.

The other group that afforded me a great deal of support, the Mountain Group, was quite different. My participation started after I got a call from a friend, another local entrepreneur. I believe we'd met at a Chamber of Commerce mixer. In a place like Burlington, Vermont, you got to know all the local business owners. And in the early '80s, northern Vermont was a hotbed of burgeoning businesses. Ben & Jerry's had started in an old, deserted gas station on the corner of College and St. Paul Street—the bottom of the street where I lived. I remember going in there when they first opened and thinking, "This will never last." Boy, was I wrong! Other innovative businesses were born there as well—BioTek, Burton, Seventh Generation, Gardener's Supply, and Magic Hat Brewery. Later, Green Mountain

Coffee, and Dealer.com came along. Yes, Burlington and its environs were rife with creative entrepreneurs.

So, one day, my phone rang and it was John, one of my entrepreneurial friends. He and his partners owned one of the more prestigious building companies in the area.

"Lisa, listen, who do you talk to?"

"Whatever do you mean?" I asked with a laugh.

"I mean, as an owner, the boss—who do we get to riff off at? How do I know how much to pay myself? If I'm getting the best insurance for my situation? Who can I talk to about that who doesn't want to charge me dollars for the privilege? My partners and I have been talking about this. Wives, partners—it's not enough. I've been talking with some other people, other biz owners, and we agree. We've actually met a couple of times now—me, Ben Cohen from the ice cream place, Will from Gardener's—you know these people. We've started meeting, and it's been great! We get to talk about our business concerns and challenges with peers who aren't invested, who have a different perspective, but come from a similar vantage point."

I totally understood. I didn't have anyone to take my problems home to at night but understood the issues of discussing business with a partner and with paid consultants. To have peers—with no attachment to any outcomes, yet willing to listen and offer their ideas—what an interesting concept. And to also hear what they were up against . . . But John was going on.

"So, in thinking about the goals and organization of this group, we thought we should have a woman—a woman's voice. And, well, I thought of you. Interested?"

Before I could respond, he continued "We will meet once a month and rotate hosting. The host gets to pick the topic. We can either meet at the host's business or a restaurant, if that's more private. Whaddaya think?"

"I am in!" I said without hesitation.

Once a month, this group of entrepreneurial peers—we called ourselves the Mountain Group—would meet. Our members shifted through the times and tides of business and personal demands. Ben Cohen and Jerry Greenfield were early attendees but didn't last long. Bill Schubart was there when he was head of Resolution (he's now a writer and NPR contributor). Will Raap (of Gardener's Supply) was always a thoughtful contributor, and Alan Newman (serial entrepreneur: Gardener's Supply, Seventh Generation, Magic Hat Brewery) was always fun when he came—he liked to incite a bit of mischief, if I recall correctly. I invited Hinda to join as well. We were the token women for a very long time. In our gatherings, we discussed everything from our own compensation rates, employee issues, ESOPs, quality control, and balancing our personal goals with business goals. We were socially conscious up-and-comers. And of course we drank, ate well, and had fun.

Meanwhile, our Jogbra business just kept growing . . .

As a result, our rent kept increasing as we took over more and more space on the mill's third floor for warehousing and shipping. It was our CFO, Dave, or our accountant, or someone in the Mountain Group, or perhaps Hinda's father—or maybe all of the above—who at some point around this time asked the crucial question: "Why are you still paying rent at Mill Street?" It turned out that we were now in a position to build a building for our Jogbra company and could become our own landlords—rather than pay rent to a third party, we could pay the rent to ourselves!

We found a small industrial park in Williston, Vermont with an affordable lot. It was just east of Burlington, beyond Winooski, where we were in The Mill. Williston had, for centuries, been typical Vermont farmland. It sprawled across a large area of fields and gentle hills. Even in 1988, it still had only a small village center with the requisite gas pump, general store, and nearby white-steepled church. On one of its edges, there was a horse farm holding down a corner of the one and only large intersection that came into the south end of the area, far from the village center. But Williston was morphing from agriculture to industry—with trucking, warehousing, and light industrial enterprises springing up. The small family farms were disappearing. Within a decade of Jogbra's arrival in the area, that very visible horse farm on the corner would be replaced by housing and a mall—complete with a Christmas Shoppe, grocery store, restaurants, and a movie theater.

Jogbra contributed to this supposed progress in Williston when we built our building there. The industrial park we chose was on the western edge of town, where its commercial growth had begun. It was the area nearest to Burlington. There were obvious advantages: We were closer to the airport. It was easier for trucks to get in and out. Did I mention how hard it was getting inventory up and down all those flights in our Mill Street location? And employee parking was no longer a concern. But we were in an industrial park, and no longer able to just walk out the door and get a coffee, or lunch, or go window-shopping while thinking over a problem. There was no lovely river to gaze at, just other industrial facades. It would be a big change.

We had more fun than frustrations, I think, designing and building that space—even though it was basically a huge warehouse with an office area attached to its front. We discovered soon enough that what we needed was a rather formulaic architectural plan—nothing had to be reinvented. We had no problem getting a commercial mortgage, which was handled primarily by our CFO, Dave. But, as the building neared completion—and because we were us and had to have our stamp on the building—we built a basically nonfunctional lattice enclosure around the front entrance and planted climbing roses at its base. I was concerned with aesthetics, with bringing beauty into my surroundings. It was my artist-consciousness, still making itself known under my entrepreneur-girl-boss persona.

When it came time to decorate individual offices, the difference between Hinda's and mine showcased our opposite personalities. Hinda's office was on the front side of the building, on the northeastern corner, and looked out over the parking lot. She chose a very hip and modern, gray, stippled/sponge paint job for her walls, with a decorative geometric motif hand stenciled in mauves periodically at about hip height. I think her carpet was a deep burgundy-purple. She ordered a large gray-topped table for her desk. It was very modern, sophisticated, and sleek.

I chose an office across the hall from Hinda, on the back side of the allotted office area, because it had windows that faced east, and I loved the morning sunlight. I painted the walls white and laid a dark-green rug. I was going for a sort of "bring the outdoors in" effect.

I finally returned my grandfather's big, old, oak desk to a room at home and bought a brand new, modern white desk and matching bookshelves. Houseplants were the finishing touch. I put some artwork on the walls—some mine, but mostly others' prints, primarily florals. I also put a white wicker couch against the wall across from my desk, padded with floral cushions. It's where I would go pre- or post-seizure. Which, I hasten to add, was less often. I only needed such lay-downs or recuperations a couple of times during the entire time I occupied that office.

We moved into our new digs in April of 1988 and had a big office-warming party to celebrate. Oh, we had fun! The champagne flowed. The table in the conference room was laden with goodies, as were a few tables in the warehouse shipping area. Hinda and I took turns giving tours of the new space, which usually entailed explaining how the warehouse and shipping area operated. My sister came from California to attend and helped organize my new office. Norine came up from New York City—not only as one of our star sales reps, but as a friend. All of our various business associates came, as did many of the Mountain Group members. Most of our employees brought their significant others. We invited everyone. I felt a deep sense of accomplishment. The baby was grown-up and had her own home.

We were getting a lot of publicity in magazines like *Glamour* and on the cover of *Entrepreneur.* Newspapers like *USA Today* also gave us coverage. Most importantly, we were always hearing from women who were wearing our products. We received thank you notes, suggestions, criticisms, general feedback, and lots of their stories.

Hence those many animated discussions around the table during the managers' meetings, or at the Sandage Advertising & Marketing office, or with a sales rep over a glass of wine after calling on accounts. Evolution was afoot, and despite the long hours, often mundane travel destinations, and the inevitable setbacks, we were excited, enthralled, challenged, and committed.

I was beginning to understand it wasn't just about selling sports bras anymore. Though I struggled to articulate it at the time, I knew I had to stretch outside my comfort zone. I knew I had to keep growing. However, I did not yet realize that my little invention was becoming a facilitator for so many other girls and women to also be able to challenge their own perceived barriers.

Around this time, in 1988, the TV sitcom *Murphy Brown* started airing. I devoured it. Watching it back in those days, I guess I was looking for cues about how to be who I was attempting to be: a strong woman boss, with a twist of sorts—not quite traditional, paving new ways, trying to deal with my inconsistencies. But Murphy was many things I was not. She struck me as a sort of Hinda-Lisa blend, what we might be at our combined best: capable, smart, irascible, sometimes difficult, sometimes funny, but always getting things done and taking no prisoners, all for the higher good. Well, that was my private fantasy, anyway. I knew I cared far more than Murphy about how others felt, how I was perceived, and whether others were happy. Nonetheless, I looked at what she was wearing, how she bucked the establishment, and dealt with her single status. I noticed that her acerbic attitude aside, her ethics and values were similar to mine. In the end, she made me laugh and not feel quite so isolated.

As the business grew, so did our public personae. Sandage was good at getting us press, eventually hiring someone exclusively to do public relations and publicity for their accounts—but probably mainly Jogbra. Usually the PR emphasis was on women being in business, which was still remarkable enough in that time to sell newspapers and magazines. Sometimes a degree of attention would be paid on the importance of the product itself. But, in truth, it was the novelty factor at first, with the sports bra's significance and impact only becoming noticed as the years—and results—were catalogued.

Shortly after we had moved into the new building on Avenue D, I got a surprising phone call. It was an editor at *People* magazine. They'd heard about a woman with epilepsy who had her own bra company, and wondered if maybe there was a human-interest story in it for them—was I interested? *People* magazine! Wow! My rag mag of choice! I think Hinda even had a subscription. Of course, I was way flattered. It would be my fifteen minutes of fame. I said yes. They told me they were on a hard deadline, and their crew would arrive the next day to interview me and take the photos. Would that be convenient? I cleared my calendar. And what did I think of first? I was in a tizzy about what to wear. On such short notice, there was no time to shop. And I told everyone in the office, "It's *People*

magazine! We must tidy up! They're going to take photos."
We were all excited, and ran around staging my office, the
reception area—anywhere we thought they might decide
to shoot.

The next morning, I applied my makeup ever so carefully and fussed over my unruly, curly hair obsessively.
I forget what I finally decided to wear. A small group of
people arrived and trooped down the hall to my office,
where they assembled just outside my door. I invited them
all in, but the one woman who seemed to be in charge, after
giving me and my office a swift and brief gaze, dismissed
the guys with cameras and told them to go back down the
hall to scout out good photo-op areas. Then, she came into
my office. We exchanged pleasantries and got underway
with what I had come to consider the usual questions. At
one point, I asked her if she would like to meet my business
partner.

"Partner? You have a business partner?" the interviewer
asked.

"Um, yes!" I think I might have done a double take.
"Yes." Hadn't the magazine done its research before sending a passel of people to Vermont?

"Where is this partner?"

"Across the hall. Would you like to meet her?" I got up
and walked around my desk. We walked across to Hinda's
office where, once the introductions were made, the *People*
interviewer said, "I have to make a call." She vanished into

the hall. Hinda and I stood together in her office looking at one another in confusion.

"What just happened?" Hinda asked.

"I have no idea." I shrugged my shoulders, and we both sat down. Hinda went back to whatever was in front of her on her desk, and after a moment I got up and wandered back into my own office.

A few moments, later the interviewer came back down to my office with the photographers trailing behind her. I looked up at her expectantly.

"We have to leave," she announced. "This isn't the story."

I might have said something eloquent like, "Huh?"

The woman explained that she'd phoned in and they didn't know I had a business partner. So it just wasn't the story they thought it was going to be, so they were leaving. Sorry.

"What about the story that it is?" I asked.

"Not my call, Lisa. Sorry."

She turned around with her coterie and left the scene.

End of story. I never made it into *People* magazine.

There were lots of interviews and bits of publicity events. This incident with *People* happened to be one of the funnier, odder ones, and one that surely accents the famous "fickle finger of fate"—or, in this case, fame.

In addition to Jogbra, I'd been asked to make promotional videos for the Epilepsy Foundation, and they'd given me their national award. All this brought up the issue of ego. Or "fame is Viagra for the ego," as I came to write years later. *What is a healthy ego, and what is an inflated one? A detrimental sense of self?* I really did think about this a lot. I was overwhelmed and humbled by my discovery and experiences with the Epilepsy Foundation and its community. Their recognition, and my ability to make a difference there, was a newfound amazement. Although perceived as "successful," I felt a fraud in the sporting goods community. And being virtually married to this business had shanghaied all my creative juices from artistic pursuits to commerce—not to mention sabotaged my attempts at having an actual marriage to a human.

Should I be believing, I wondered, *my own press?*

We had really arrived. But somewhere deep inside, I was listening to advice I was giving others when I would speak at some event or class: "You make your plans looking upward toward your goal, only to reach it and find that what you thought was the pinnacle, the ceiling of your endeavor, was in fact only the floor of your next level . . ."

21.

REFLECTIONS

"It's on the strength of observation and reflection that one finds a way. So we must dig and delve unceasingly."
~ Claude Monet

One autumnal day in 1988, I was sitting in my fancy new office on Avenue D when a phone call came in that unsettled me. It was an old UVM classmate I hadn't seen in over a decade calling to ask for a charitable contribution. Although I received such calls rather frequently, what made this one different was that toward the end she asked if I was still writing poetry. This not only took me aback—it took me back in *time*. Here was a person whose last experience of me was that of artist and writer. I found myself fumbling for an answer.

It had been over a dozen years since I had broken up my stained-glass studio, folded up my easel, and put away my oil paints. At the time, my friends, mostly artists, had asked with incredulity, "How can you go from being an artist to a businessperson?" They almost spat out the word "business," as if just saying it was somehow a defilement. But I'd found starting a business extremely challenging and exciting—a daily learning experience that stretched me enormously. In the early days, it had definitely been a creative process.

During my early college years, I'd taken a course at UVM that explored the nature of the creative process—a very '70s kind of curriculum item. The text was a compilation of writings by recognized creative thinkers: Albert Einstein, Vincent Van Gogh, Friedrich Nietzsche, and Carl Jung, to name a few. Each one, quite independently, recounted similar experiences of the creative process, drawing similar conclusions. To wit, that it begins with vision and boils down to problem-solving. Creative thinking looks at all the different ways there are to solve a problem and then applies the best way.

In art, this is found in composition, light, color, and their relationship—these are all elements of a puzzle to be "solved" or put together, often with several different workable solutions that the artist will try. It's a delightful puzzle that can go together in an infinite amount of combinations, limited only by the individual's imagination, and surely stamped with it.

During the start-up phase of my business, while it had been a shock to my friends, my career change didn't seem all that radical to me. I was simply applying my creative process to a different medium: commerce. But often, in the evening, I would pick up a pen and write away. Some weekends I would paint. Slowly, those urges diminished.

Finally, I was left only with a reputation in the office of being an irrepressible doodler, covering pages and pages of yellow pads, spreadsheets, and meeting agendas with what was left of the "artistic" manifestation of my creative abilities.

When I heard my ex-classmate's question, I felt guilty, ashamed. She, after all, had managed to integrate her art into her mode of making a living. Had I?

After we hung up, I sat at my desk, reflecting. What had happened to my creative process? It had all been channeled into the endeavor of first creating and then maintaining and running a business. And it occurred to me that the product was rather abstract—a successful business. These days, there were no creative juices left in me by the time I got home at night. I felt disappointed in myself. If I tried to review my day and see where those juices went, I saw the puzzle of a business: sales strategies, budget crunching, people management, and product extensions.

Was I still an artist—working in the medium of money, creating commerce? Had the canvas become industry, the paints our products, and the brushes our employees? The scorecard did not lie with the critics' aesthetic acclaim, but in profit and loss statements. The real question for me was one of worthiness. We live in a culture that lionizes the pursuit of the dollar and dismisses the importance of art.

Somewhere along the modern cultural storyline, artists got characterized as being rather self-indulgent, eccentric, and irresponsible, while the words most often associated with a businessperson are more along the lines of "serious," "contributor," "hardworking," and "responsible."

Where was all my reflection leading me? I wanted to discover the truth beyond the stereotypes—to examine the daily applications of my creative energy and judge, for myself, their "worthiness." My worthiness.

I wanted to discover what really matters.

22.
WHO ARE WE?

"It's difficult to believe in yourself because the idea
of self is an artificial construction. You are, in
fact, part of the glorious oneness of the universe.
Everything beautiful in the world is within you."
~ Russell Brand

I remember being at a very large national sporting goods show. It was at some point in the "Gravy '80s" and we were quite successful by then and well known in the industry. I recall walking around the noisy, people-filled convention center exchanging waves with busy acquaintances, nodding to others as I passed. The aisles were lined with booths aggressively selling everything from athletic clothing to fishing rods, dartboards, and beyond. Every athletic shoe manufacturer was there. The place was a sparkling mosaic of color, bustling with people and commerce.

And as I took in the scene I was wondering, *How the hell had I ended up here?* I felt a complete fraud, with nothing in common with all these enthusiastic jocks and jockettes. The choices that brought me here had made sense at the time and, upon reflection, still seemed to stand true.

The ironies were not lost on me. They are not lost on me still. One of the most authentic aspects of myself, the meditative runner, had spawned this persona of sporting goods queen. The Jogbra Lady. It follows me to this day.

The further irony being that I could no longer be that runner—two bad knees that no surgery could fix. No activity—not bodysurfing, not walking—fulfilled me as running did. I miss it to this day.

But then I read an article that purported that many who gain rapid success feel "like a fraud," believing that somehow they are pulling off a grand illusion that could be "found out" by others. I know I felt that way, especially in those early Jogbra years. I wasn't a jock! I didn't run in races! Then, I wasn't even a runner anymore! Egad!

Hindsight is a powerful tool when we choose to use it. It is an easy form of perspective, available to all who care to look. Although I haven't done a formal review and tally, my observations suggest that almost every spiritual teacher offers some way of engaging with what is a truly powerful learning mechanism: hindsight, reflection.

Life has shown me that the "Who Am I?" exercise I experienced years ago at the Human Factors retreat is really more about the *we*.

Who was I in the 1980s? Was I Lisa the epileptic? The inventor of the sports bra? A difficult business partner? Woman? Human? Particle of the cosmos?

When I was all done being "the Jogbra Lady," as so many people still refer to me, I asked myself, "What really matters? I mean, what *really* matters?"

The answer, surprisingly, was beauty—the experience of true, authentic beauty. Not what passes for beauty in our culture these days—no, that's glamour, and glamour is an illusion, a trick that doesn't last. True beauty is eternal.

And although it felt right, I had no idea what that answer meant. I knew I had to find out. And upon reflection, through that lens of hindsight, it was apparent that Lisa the Seeker had always been there and was still alive and—well, *seeking.* And that being an entrepreneur was a powerful and often efficient way to seek.

The "Who Am I?" exercise leads the participant to the realization of our common divinity. We may not all need to sit in exercises for hours. Sometimes just hearing the truth is enough: We are individuated nodes on the whole. We are *one.*

And it is True Beauty that holds us all together in its web of harmony.

23.

THE BEGINNING
OF THE END

*"For time and the world do not stand still. Change
is the law of life. And those who look only to the past
or the present are certain to miss the future."*
~ John F. Kennedy

In midsummer of 1989, I was sitting at my desk when my phone buzzed. When Mary Jane, my administrative assistant, told me who was on the line, I was surprised. It was a guy who had been our buyer many years ago at JCPenney™, during our short-lived experiment into private labeling. Quick aside: therein lies another tale of "lesson learned"—build your own brand, not someone else's.

I hadn't heard from this guy in years, so I wondered what precipitated his call.

"Hey, hello, stranger!" I said when I picked up the phone. There was a smile in my voice because, though our business goals hadn't meshed, we had gotten along well and I had enjoyed working with him.

"Hi, Lisa! How are you? I know the Jogbra business is doing well; I see it everywhere! But how are *you*?"

I laughed and answered, and we started catching up. I learned he had left JCPenney™ and was no longer a buyer. He was now in a different capacity with another company, Playtex™ Apparel. Then he got down to the reason for his call.

"Clearly, you are growing by leaps and bounds. I'm sure that is creating some challenges." He went on to extol the virtues of the Playtex™ company and brand, among other things, saying, "and we are always interested in meeting our customers' needs. To that end, I'm wondering if, perhaps, there is any way we might help each other out."

At that point in my career, I didn't yet know that this was a sort of code phrase. "Perhaps you might come down to New York? We can discuss ways we might be able to *help* one another."

It seems silly now, and somewhat inconceivable, that I was so naïve. I really did not know, did not admit to myself, what was really being suggested in those pithy few sentences. I knew something was brewing, but I did not understand what.

We had always been able to finance Jogbra's astounding growth internally, primarily using the device of bank debt in the form of a revolving line of credit. But we kept growing. And financing a 25 percent growth rate per annum in years one through five is far more doable than in the more sales-laden years five through ten. We were facing a whole new level of sophistication on the financial front. Financing was getting complicated. The bank wanted everything to get more complicated. Hinda and I were looking at the probability of having to take on some serious debt together in order to keep our baby growing in response to the continuing demand.

We talked briefly about our choices, other alternatives. But this was in the days before easy initial public offerings, or "IPOs." Such a move was unheard of for a company our size in that era. Other entrepreneurial companies we knew of were dealing with similar issues by sharing ownership with employees. A relatively new idea at the time, also complicated, but it brought the whole discussion of "selling" to the forefront once again. It was something we had to look at.

And then that phone call came.

I got on a plane and went down to have lunch in New York with my old buyer friend and another gentleman from Playtex™, who turned out to be an attorney. Over Caesar salad and sparkling water with lemon, it became clear to me that Playtex™ Apparel was interested in buying Jogbra Sports Bras.

It took almost an entire year for the deal to come to fruition. And many, many "expert" opinions and valuations. There was also a great deal of very difficult secrecy.

It is no lie when I say that if starting and running my own business was the equivalent of getting my MBA, then selling it was equal to receiving my PhD. The courtship, negotiations, soul-searching, and series of decisions that comprised the act of selling Jogbra were monumental in and of themselves. Each phase revealed the necessity for new levels of endeavor, deeper grasp of self-awareness, and clearer understandings of my (true) goals.

And, oh, hey! "You can't tell anyone what's going on 'til it's a done deal." We were told not to mention it to friends, family, or employees—no one. This was so not easy for me. I just discussed it with my cat, my shrink, and Hinda, of course.

The decision to sell was a difficult one for me, and I believe for Hinda as well—though I think for different reasons. To better understand our options and our resources, we hired a consultant whose specialty was counseling businesses on whether to sell—and, if so, how and for how much. Ed Kiniry became our sounding board and guide through this unknown territory. A territory in which we were not even sure we wanted to travel, let alone arrive at a destination—the sale of our company. But we embarked, nonetheless, on the journey—curious, as ever, and willing to be educated. Our company was growing and needed to be fed, meaning it needed more money. In my heart, I knew I did not want to get more deeply bound to this partnership, which is what new debt would ensure. I was willing to explore selling Jogbra and consider seriously letting go.

For some time now, the game had been different. It was no longer primarily about creation and *becoming*. By 1989 Jogbra was too much about profit and loss, retained earnings, beating the competition. It seemed to me that my work was more about *maintenance* and *protection* than it was about *creation*. I was making more than enough money, putting fully half of every paycheck into savings and still living quite comfortably. In my heart of hearts, I was ready to move on, get back to being Lisa the artist, stop being married to the business, and maybe have time to find a human mate.

Playtex™ made us several offers, or more accurately, several versions of their offer. I learned the difference between a stock deal and a cash deal. I learned about payout options and all the permutations of the attendant tax consequences dependent upon which flavor of deal one was perusing. With our accountant and consultant, we pored over each one as it came in, dissected and discussed it. We rejected each in turn.

Weeks went by. Then months.

During the negotiations, we met with the three main actors on the Playtex™ Apparel stage. I don't recall all their titles; Hercules Sotos was the financial guy, Donald

Franceschini was president, and Joel Smilow was the big cheese. They all made a point of meeting Hinda and me and assessing us, which I took as standard operating procedure. Of the three, Don seemed to be in charge of us and this deal. It was he who called me when calling was necessary. He was the relationship guy; he showed me photos of his family and home. I noticed that he smiled easily.

Our consultant, Ed, was getting exasperated with us. He was done being politic, polite. We'd worn out the learning curve as an excuse. Our indecisiveness was no longer okay. "You two can't keep stringing Playtex™ along! They are not going to continue to be so patient! Decide *if* you want to sell, and then if you really do, determine what your magic number is and we'll present the offer. Otherwise, ladies, it is time to let this go."

I knew I was ready to see what "the rest of my life" could be about, given an equitable way to exit this chapter. I had arrived at my decision: I was ready to sell. But Hinda seemed to be dragging her feet.

Frankly, I was mystified as to why Playtex™ wanted to buy us. Every other "traditional" bra company had just come up with their own version of a sports bra. Why hadn't the makers of the famous 18-Hour Bra™ done the same? Why purchase our company? It would be a couple of years before I discovered what I believed to be the answer.

But at that moment, I wasn't thinking too much about their motives—only my own.

Hinda and I took Ed's advice to heart and devised a plan—a rather clever one, even if basic. We agreed that we would each come up with our own magic "I'll sell!" number without consulting each other. We'd see if we were even on the same page. We would give ourselves a couple of weeks. It wasn't that we hadn't discussed this before. What was unique about it this time is that after learning all the different ways the deal could be structured, all the different considerations that may affect that final number, *this* time the number we each came up with would be what we wanted to walk away with, after taxes, after the biz debt was accounted for. Playtex™ could then work backward however they needed to in order to have us each end up with our magic number.

And so, on the appointed day, I went into Hinda's office and sat down at her table. We each unfolded our little piece of paper with our thought-through magic number scrawled on it. Shockingly, we each had written down the exact same number!

Did you think I was going to say what it was? Well, no. The important bit is that we could agree: if Playtex™ could figure out how we might walk away from our "baby," each with that amount of money in our purses, then we had a deal.

I made the phone call to Don, Playtex™ Apparel's president. He allowed that our approach was a bit unorthodox, "But then, that's you two, isn't it! That's why you are up there in Vermont and I'm down here in New York, right? I'll take it back to our table and see what I can do." He hung up the phone.

Not long after, on a dark Vermont December afternoon, Don called me back and, after hellos, simply said, "You got a deal! Merry Christmas."

I think all the blood in my body drained to my feet. I definitely had a full-body reaction to the news. He chuckled, said he'd be in touch, and said good-bye. I mumbled some sort of "thanks" and "good-bye" and hung up the phone. It was a very brief, straight-to-the-point call.

I sat there for only a few seconds before vaulting out of my chair, around my desk, and across the hall into Hinda's office. Luckily, she was there, sitting at her desk—I don't know what I would have done if she hadn't been there. I closed the door behind me, walked over to where she was sitting and said, "Don just called me." She looked up quickly, her eyes bright. "We've got our deal, Hinda. *Our* deal!"

Hinda jumped up, whooped, and came around her desk, and we hugged.

But that wasn't the end; it was just the beginning. Having agreed, it was another eight months before the actual papers were signed and before the burdensome secrecy was finally over.

I was very uncomfortable for the first half of 1990. No one could know that we were doing this deal. We were told it would create too much anxiety among our employees, who, between the office and warehouse, now numbered around one hundred. Not to mention our independent sales reps in the field and our customers. Evidently sharing the information of this possible change of ownership would jeopardize the business—employees, afraid for their jobs, might leave; established dealers might reconsider their relationship with us; and potential new sales might stall in a "wait and see" mode. I found myself having to keep this secret, no matter how difficult.

When the "due diligence" phase came around, their people—lawyers and accountants, mostly—had to make sure that we were what we said we were and our numbers were legit. In this largely pre-computer era, this meant personal visits and much paper shuffling. Jogbra staff wanted to know what all the suits were doing at our offices.

Something occurred during this time that was significant. As part of the due diligence process, it came to the attention of the Playtex™ organization's legal team that there had once been another original shareholder—Polly. For some legal-schmegal reason, they required that she sign a document affirming she wouldn't make any claims in the pending deal. I didn't really understand their concern, as this was about eight years after Polly had sold her shares back to us. This upset me, nonetheless. I was told I had no choice—it was required. So, document in hand, I flew down to New York to see her.

Both Polly and I were surprised by this request—and offended. We each dislike confrontation. While the Jogbra saga had been difficult for both of us, we had weathered it, continuing to travel together, go to each other's family events, and console one another through the various other dramas life inevitably provided. But this! It pricked the old wound. It was a tense, difficult meeting, but Polly signed the document. Sometime later, I received a letter from my wonderful, quiet friend. She articulated her upset. It was difficult for me to read.

Friends—we are such teachers for each other.

There was one employee we had to let in on what was going on. It would be impossible to open our financial books to anyone without our CFO helping, directing, and knowing what was going on. And here, again, we were blessed.

Like any growing company, we'd continually improved the quality of our personnel as we grew. Nowhere was that truer than on the financial side of Jogbra, which was not a simple operation. Owning both raw and finished inventory, that was both off-site and in-house, and having salespeople on commission was a lot to juggle on the books. Tracking sales and discounts, keeping up with a significant payroll and, all the while, managing and maintaining our relationship with the bank—well, these were just part of the job description. I had discovered that while I was not so good at arithmetic (thank goodness for calculators), I got profit and loss statements and balance sheets. I just needed someone to prepare, review, and interpret them with me. I considered our financial health as Jogbra's report card. I had little inkling, back then, about the larger, social impact this product was having on the culture and the lives of women and girls.

By the time our sales were in the multimillions—a big deal back in the 1980s—we had found and hired Dave Bergeron, who was an excellent CFO. He had previously owned, operated, and sold his own business. He'd been its financial head, and when we found him, he wanted a break from ownership. He wanted to work for someone else. Our entrepreneurial venture was perfect for him—and he for us. I learned a great deal from Dave while he was on the Jogbra team.

At this point in our story, he was well aware of the looming need for capital to fund our continually climbing sales growth. Still, it was with both trepidation and relief that I called Dave into my office in early January of 1990. When Hinda and I told him about our acceptance of the Playtex™ offer, he didn't miss a beat. He recognized this as the culmination of the entrepreneurial endeavor. He knew what needed to happen next and his essential role in it. And he confirmed the great need to keep our news quiet.

"It could still go south, you know. Until all the due diligence is done—and that can take months—until all

the lawyers and accountants have done their thing and i's are dotted and t's are crossed, you don't know that this is gonna happen. You don't want to rock the boat until then."
I was so amazed and relieved to have such a knowledgeable ally on our team.

"In fact," he went on with a grin, "wait till the check clears!" And he laughed. If he'd been the sort to hug, I would have given him a hug.

It was the beginning of the end of Jogbra—at least as a private company. As *my* company.

The check cleared. The secret was made public. The suits were in my office.

I attempted to lighten the news by handing out T-shirts to the staff with Kennedy's quote: "Change is the law of life. And those who look only to the past or the present are certain to miss the future." It didn't go far. But action takes over. We all had to "jump to!" as the guys with ties arrived. After the announcements had been made, the dust settled, and fears somewhat calmed, the post-sale era for Jogbra began. The traditional corporate America style invaded the "by women for women" entrepreneurial realm we had created there in the Green Mountains of Vermont.

Often, Hinda and I had referred to the Jogbra business as "our baby." We both knew it was a growing entity that we were raising, guiding. From her birth, infancy, and all those dramatic growth spurts, we were the parental units who were fussing, arguing, worrying, and exclaiming over her growth, popularity, and integrity. Was she at the top of her class? Did we have the right tutors, dance teachers? Was she fat this year, or lean? But we'd gotten to the place where we could no longer support her, meet the demands of her ever-growing constituency, so to speak. And then there was this suitor—a suitable suitor with the required dowry—and so we had said, "Yes."

Soon, the suits were in everyone's office.

Part of the acquisition deal was that Jogbra would stay in Vermont and that few, if any, jobs would be at risk. This turned out to be true. Hinda and I had signed employment contracts as part of the deal, to oversee a smooth transition.

It soon became clear, however, that Hinda and I held very different views about what this sale meant to the Jogbra brand and, more specifically, how to move through this transition. I felt that the people we were dealing with had much to learn from us. After all, they had not dealt with the sporting goods distribution channel before. Of course, we had a great deal to learn about the Playtex™ systems, and they knew more about bras, department and lingerie store sales, and selling than we did. But as far as the Jogbra brand in sporting goods? *We* had created that. And they were not listening. I was becoming concerned about the integrity of our brand, something we had worked so hard to build.

Perhaps I was naïve.

In particular, I remember one instance about a rack program for in-store merchandising. Corporate was proposing a large metal rack, a size not sensitive to our smaller dealers. They also wanted to lacquer it using nonbrand colors. I protested, laying out my case. Hinda, when asked, did not back me up—not at all. I realized she had made a decision about where the power had shifted.

The person that Playtex™ put in charge of the transition—an elderly gentleman they'd brought on specifically for the task—decided to play Hinda and me against one another. Given our history, this was not difficult. He would use ridicule and sarcasm to get my goat, while at the same time flattering Hinda. Once, he'd even made a comment to me about Hinda: "I've always had a soft spot for redheaded Jewesses!" I didn't know which to be more flabbergasted about—that he had actually stated his preference out loud and blatantly referenced her faith *or* that he perceived Hinda as a redhead!

What I did know was that my life with my baby, Jogbra, was now over. I definitely couldn't live with her new in-laws.

Part of our deal in selling to Playtex™ was for Hinda and me to each sign a one-year employment contract. When the first year was up, they offered to continue my employment with a nice raise, but I was not eager to accept. The transition had been more difficult than I'd anticipated. The disrespect and game playing I had experienced had been far too distasteful. But what to do? Stay or leave?

My decision was not one I made quickly or easily. I agonized over it for weeks. I made lists of pros and cons. I went back and forth. My journal from this time is full of these types of conversations with myself. I had no mentor or coach on the outside to help me think through everything. My therapist was crucial in terms of helping me to emotionally survive the undercutting shenanigans I was experiencing on the job. But she knew little of the stuff of corporate playbooks.

I did talk to my Mountain Group compatriots about this. By this time, we had been meeting monthly for a few years, and we had all bonded over our respective businesses' blessings and crises. I expressed my dilemma and recorded their comments and advice in my journal. This is a sampling of what they advised:

Bill: The energy, force, dynamics of an acquisition has a life of its own and you are being pulled along with it— you're helpless. Don't beat yourself up.

Burr: Be neutral. Say your piece but be neutral.

Will: Be bold for the next sixty days.

Consensus from all: Get out and move on.

The various factors informing my thought process were simple: the ongoing difficulties with the man Playtex™ had assigned to oversee the transition, my business partner's increased and intense competition with me within this new corporate paradigm, and my urge to nurture my creative life once again. Ideally, I wanted to keep doing what I was good at—the marketing, PR, and advertising—and leave the rest of it to the new owners. I also wanted to continue being the "face" of the Jogbra brand along with Hinda. It occurred to me that I could just do just that. I could keep my hand in in those areas where I knew I excelled, work just three days a week, and still get a paycheck, albeit reduced. I proposed my part-time consulting position to corporate.

Donald Franceschini was amenable when I floated this concept but warned me that I would be giving up quite a few perks by ceasing to be a full-time executive. For one thing, I would no longer be eligible for the Playtex™ executive employees' stock purchase plan. I didn't think much about this. I thought I had figured out my "new life" with my now grown-up baby and my new corporate in-laws. I thought I was so clever to have elected to take this middle road and not leave entirely, moving into a part-time consulting position. I could have it all. Boy, was I wrong. The next few months were a torturous lesson.

Very shortly after I finally made the transition to part-time and given up my stock options, Playtex™ Apparel sold itself to Sara Lee™. This meant my Playtex™ stock, had I stayed as full-time and bought in, would have morphed into much, much, *much* more than my initial investment.

At the time, I didn't blink. I was out. I had made the choice to walk away from what was, for me, a toxic environment. Now, I look back and think, *I was so unprepared.* I was the lamb in the lions' den.

I sincerely thought I would continue to contribute—that in this specified, narrow lane, my participation would be welcomed, considered worthwhile. I thought that now that I had "conceded," the cruel, competitive plays would end. This was not the case. In fact, quite the opposite occurred. I found myself entirely written off by all parties. I became completely disempowered. Meetings about marketing—my supposed area of responsibility—were planned for days I was scheduled to be out of the office. I overheard derogatory comments made about me. Vital information wasn't shared with me, leaving me unable to remain pertinent or relevant. Even my office was given to someone else.

Reading my journal entries of 1991, which detail this dynamic as it unfolded week after week for months, is still painful. At the time, I questioned myself constantly. Were the others right? Did I have nothing left to contribute to the company I had founded? Was there truth in the derogatory comments? It was all more fodder for my overactive internal review system. I suppose it was probably Corporate Behavior 101, and I was simply too naïve to expect or identify it. Finally, I got the message: vacate the premises, shut my mouth, and just cash the paycheck until the contract ran its course.

It was a brutal ending.

When I made my decision to leave at the end of my part-time employment contract, Don came up to Vermont to speak with me. He wanted to know why I was leaving. I liked Don, and I told him the truth, but not the whole truth. I told him the part about getting back to my artist's roots, back into the studio, and seeing what else life had to offer. I did not tell him about the bullbaiting, the backstabbing, or Hinda's competition with me for his approval and that of other higher-ups in the company. But I tipped my cards, I'm afraid, when the two of us went into Hinda's office to tell her, officially, that I would be leaving.

We sat down and I opened the conversation by saying, "Well, Hinda, you are going to get what you have always wanted—to run Jogbra solo."

"Whoa!" Don said, and adjusted himself in his chair, looking back and forth between Hinda and me.

Hinda just smiled, saying nothing.

"Well, that says a lot!" Don continued.

I realized that with just those few words, I had revealed an element of our partnership that I don't believe the Playtex™ management team had hitherto fully ascertained. Hinda and I had, after all, been on good terms until the sale occurred. I don't know why, at that juncture, I cared one way or the other about this revelation.

When we returned to my office, Don let me know, again, that I did not have to go. He reiterated the amount of money that would be in my paycheck. I smiled and said, "Don, I will never be as wealthy as you are."

"My wealth is my family," he replied. Surprised, I liked him even more in that moment. Privately, it made me all the more aware of the fact that in order to make time and energy to have a family of *my* own, I had to leave Jogbra—the only "family" I'd been able to create to date. I was forty-two years old.

24.
TEACHERS

"The power of life comes from within; go there. Pray;
meditate. Reach for those luminous places in yourself."
~ Ardis Whitman

Curiosity. That is one of my most enduring and consistent qualities. It makes me a perennial student.

One way this curiosity manifests is that I am always open to someone else's viewpoint or worldview. I may often "try it on for size" before deciding whether to adjust or stick with my own views. It is both a blessing and a curse, infused in my psyche again by one of my mother's oft-repeated platitudes, "Walk a mile in another person's shoes before passing judgment." It was one of the reasons my first marriage, to Al, had lasted for so long. I think any other young woman would have vacated that situation years before I did. But I thought, perhaps, his concept of loving another—in its repudiation of the physical element of our marriage—was somehow higher, purer, and might somehow have validity. I thought I should try to figure out how to live with it, learn from it.

Ah, youth! Was it stupidity or stubbornness? Fearfulness? Or altruism, perhaps? But then, again, the '70s had been a confusing decade, and I'd fancied myself a seeker even then. And perhaps it was also, in part, a function of growing up in the 1950s and '60s, the youngest of four, learning by observing the older kids who were always telling me they knew what to do, how to do it best, how to do it better than me. Teaching—my siblings saw themselves as *teaching* me. My being self-referential was not encouraged.

As a young woman, I had a vivid imagination that saw many possibilities. My sense of humor responded to this with wild, sometimes crazy ideas. On the other hand, my innate sense of caution—strengthened by the constant threat of epilepsy—would step in, often putting on the brakes. It was, therefore, with a sort of horrid fascination, secret glee, and no small amount of admiration that I regarded Hinda's fearlessness in taking action. And while at times I felt she was reckless, I understood the value of her fast-paced style.

Hinda, I believe, also began to understand how our differences complemented each other. She seemed to recognize that my vision was a key driver in our continued ability to be relevant in our marketplace. I think she also came to understand how my relative ease in developing and maintaining our business relationships was integral to Jogbra's ongoing success. But after we sold our company—actually, almost the minute the suits arrived in our offices—she reverted and saw me once again only as a threat. To me, it felt like a switch had been flipped. I did not want to once again be involved in such a useless game. I was not interested in competing with her for the approval of "the boys" (as I secretly thought of them). This, more than anything else, steeled me for the departure from my business. I needed to return to a life that felt far more inherently natural, one without such contention. It would take years of therapy for me to fully understand the personal impact of that contentious and abrupt ending to such an important era in my life.

Per my pattern, I did not want to embark on the next part of my journey alone. I went looking for that "human family" to replace my "Jogbra family." I let all my friends and acquaintances know my intentions, and by the end of 1992, less than a year after leaving Jogbra, I had found the man who was to become my new husband. With his two wonderful, teenaged daughters, I acquired an "instant family." I morphed into a field-hockey stepmom and a good wife. I designed and built us a beautiful house, complete with a large art studio, in a lovely location on Lake Champlain. I created beautiful flower gardens and started writing more than just in my journals. For a while it was a sweet, magical time.

It was during this era that I did some of the most mean-ingful work of my life. I became a member of the Board of Directors for the Epilepsy Foundation of America in 1991—the first person with epilepsy to do so. I completed three terms on this board, working with them for nine years in several different capacities. But it was as chair of the Task Force on Women and Epilepsy that I was able to raise awareness to create and implement significant change. I saw the scientific community finally acknowl-edge the differences that gender could have in epilepsy and epilepsy therapies. Finally, the concerns of women patients, long overlooked and dismissed, would be taken seriously.

Until I started working in that community, having ep-ilepsy had been a largely private matter, even as CEO of Jogbra. To begin working with people who were concerned with, educated about, and familiar with epilepsy was an empowering and eye-opening experience. I learned that the stigma attached to having epilepsy was very real, not just something I'd imagined over the course of my life. I recognized how much this shadow element of "my condi-tion" had been an insidious factor in almost all of my life choices—especially when it came to interacting with other people. I tended to underplay epilepsy's influence and im-pact in my everyday actions.

It is a fact that people with epilepsy have greater diffi-culty getting and staying employed—let alone achieving financial stability. This was a large consideration for me way back in 1977 when I chose to create my own work, first as an artist, then as an entrepreneur. Through my experiences with the Epilepsy Foundation I came to appreciate just how unusual *this* epileptic person's story was. The Jogbra story is an illustration of what being "*differently* abled" can look like. My heretofore private experiences and the ways in which I managed my disability in the midst of running a rapid-growth business had the ability to inform and inspire others struggling to cope. As a result, I stepped onto the path of becoming a health advocate. I have spoken to groups about epilepsy ever since, and even filmed videos for the Foundation and educational TV.

In 1999, as my tenure on the Epilepsy Foundation's board was drawing to a close, I started a new company with Dr. Lesli Bell in response to an altogether different health issue. We designed a compression garment to address a painful and debilitating side effect afflicting breast cancer survivors. For chest and breast lymphedema, *this* bra, the "Bellisse Compressure Comfort Bra," is actually a patented medical device.

Yes, the years after leaving Jogbra were fruitful and busy.

A lifetime of managing a chronic medical condition and being an entrepreneur conspired to make me an even more dedicated student. Later, when I was able to finally return to graduate school, it was not in fine arts or business. I've learned that one teacher leads us to the next, if we are open to it—if we listen, look, and seek. And these days, we are lucky, because as the paradigm shifts, many teachers are surfacing. Technology makes them very available, and each in their own way shows us why we need not feel helpless or hopeless. To name a few that I've had the privilege to learn a bit from: the late and wondrous Barbara Marx Hubbard, Jean Shinoda Bolen, Mark Nepo, Joan Borysenko, Deepak Chopra, and Lynne McTaggart. I learned a great deal.

But I still had many lessons to learn. My second marriage, much like my first, was not growing along with me. My stepdaughters were off in jobs and college, and by our tenth anniversary, my husband and I were at odds more frequently. I found myself diminishing or stifling my creative urges. He didn't like that I'd taken up meditation. Increasingly, I felt I had to conceal what was truly important to me in order to keep the peace.

Though I'd sought out a therapist many years earlier to help me cope with that last difficult transitional year at Jogbra, I had dismissed her ultimate diagnosis of complex post-traumatic stress disorder (C-PTSD). I could not accept that I'd been so negatively affected by my years building Jogbra and by my business partnership with Hinda. At the time, I didn't understand the connections to my childhood or the repetitive traumas, both physical and emotional, due to epilepsy. Instead, I had immediately found another, different sort of cohort in my second husband and had jumped right into that partnership. But despite (and sometimes because of) what I might be doing in the outer world, I never paused my inner journey of self-examination and reflection. Through both therapy and all I was learning from my teachers, I came to understand how facing my vulnerabilities—living through them rather than denying or hiding from them—was the key not only to personal transformation, but to living a transformational life.

As the new millennium came in, I was also realizing that in too many ways my life with my second husband was a form of hiding. My insecurities about living and being alone had to be confronted. Hindsight suggests that during those years in that beautiful house on the shore of Lake Champlain, I was actually recovering from my corporate years, dealing with the C-PTSD that I'd been trying to deny, and in the process discovering who Lisa was beyond the "Jogbra Lady." While my second husband was, like me, a seeker on a spiritual path, his was quite different from the one that was unfurling in front of me. And his discomfort with my path kept increasing.

In 2006, I packed my bags, leaving my lakeside house and gardens (and husband), and headed to California to, finally, finish the graduate degree I had abandoned back at UVM in 1978. On the northern coast, just outside San Francisco, I discovered the time and place to actually study beauty. When my thesis advisor approved my topic, "The Importance of True Beauty in Our Culture," I was elated. My Master of Arts in Culture and Spirituality opened me to an amazing new world of perspectives, beginning with "The Universe Story," as ecotheologian Thomas Berry and cosmologist Brian Swimme named it. I found that my voice and pen could at last articulate what really mattered: reclaiming the experience of True Beauty.

Eventually, I discovered the Foundation for Shamanic Studies (FSS), founded by anthropologist Michael Harner. Their three-year program became the next vehicle for pursuing my inquiries into this incredible, beautiful privilege of living. It afforded me a new community of very diverse, yet like-minded seekers. Not until our third year of studying together did any of them know of my background with the sports bra.

As time has passed, I have continued to gain perspective— such an unsung blessing of the aging process. I've come to realize that my invention of the sports bra significantly helped many women and girls. My work in the epilepsy community also made a difference. The Bellisse Bra relieves suffering for many cancer survivors. And now, hopefully, going forward, my book *Beauty as Action* will gain a foothold in the current cultural psyche, for I believe its message is another game-changer.

My years of study with FSS served to further validate my understanding that our world has a soul—the concept of *anima mundi*. We are part of a conscious universe, and what we consider simply material "things" are aware, sentient beings—albeit perhaps on a very different vibratory level. Even the scientific community now has proponents within its ranks touting the following paradigm shift: that it is *consciousness* that is primary, not materiality, as modern science has believed and acted upon for so long.

It is in and of this consciousness that we experience our unity, our oneness.

25.
(R)EVOLUTION

"Driven by the forces of love, the fragments of the world
seek each other so that the world may come to being."
~ Pierre Teilhard de Chardin

I have written here primarily of the invention of the sports bra and the partnership that midwived it, brought it up, and married it off. But the Jogbra business went on to have a life and supporters that I was not privy to, much as any parent isn't privy to their adult child's life. Hinda stayed with Jogbra's new parent company for seven years after our company was sold. During her solo tenure, which lasted until 1997, I was never invited back to participate in any Jogbra events, though the company's offices remained in my hometown until 2003.

Nonetheless, somewhere along the way, I made sure to reintroduce Polly's name and contributions into the Jogbra's genesis story, especially as it became clear—through the continued press and interview requests—that the sports bra had become an iconic product with long-reaching impact on the lives of women and girls. This is something I didn't truly recognize until many years after I left Jogbra. Really, for thirty years, I had been myopic—but a growing body of work opened my eyes to the importance of what we had achieved.

In 2014, the Smithsonian Museum of American History deemed the Jogbra story and all our old photos and historical files important enough to add to their archives. The growing number of women participating in sports showed how Title IX and the sports bra had worked together to change the game for young athletic women:

> Subsequent to Title IX, women and girls have become much more involved in sports. College women's athletic participation has increased from 15% in 1972 to 43% in 2001. High school girl's athletic participation increased from 295,000 in 1971 to 2.8 million in 2002-2003, an increase of over 840%. In 2004, the average number of teams offered for females per college/university was 8.32, up from 2.50 per school in 1972 (Carpenter & Acosta, 2005). In 1981-82, women's championships became a part of the NCAA program. Today, the NCAA sponsors forty women's championships, thirty-eight men's championships, and three combined championships in all three of its divisions (NCAA, 2005).

"The Greatest Invention in Running—EVER—Is the Sports Bra" was published by *Runner's World* on August 30, 2018. Writer and runner, Erin G. Ryan, wrote this most moving tribute:

Unleash the Girls

As a woman, a feminist, and a runner, I find the sports bra fascinating and revolutionary. It's a product that came about during the height of the culture wars then known as 'women's lib'—the movement in the 1960s and '70s for equal rights and pay—and was actually designed for women's comfort during an activity that makes us feel good, not to please the male gaze . . .

The sports bra has become much more than an undergarment—it's a part of American culture. Who could forget soccer player Brandi Chastain scoring the winning goal in the 1999 Women's World Cup, ripping her shirt off, kneeling on the pitch, and roaring in her sports bra like a warrior? Or the role of the sports bra in street fashion, from TLC to Aaliyah to Rihanna? Athleisure, anyone? . . .

But more importantly, the sports bra has had an immeasurable, cumulative impact in the lives of ordinary women. Without a garment designed to support our bodies properly, millions of us wouldn't have taken up running. And running has become the foundation of what makes so many of us feel confident and formidable. If I can run 5, 10, 26, 50 miles, who's to tell me I can't switch careers, move to a new city, tackle motherhood, persevere through tragedy and loss? To run is to prove to yourself that you can.

In our personal lives, careers, and even in our political rights, things can be taken from us—by bad judgment, bad luck, or other forces beyond our control. But not in running. Every mile run is a mile that cannot be erased, every finish line crossed is a line that cannot be uncrossed. It may be an undergarment that started as two jockstraps sewn together in

Vermont, but by enabling women to run, the sports bra has given us access to indelible achievements. It's given us power beyond the fleeting bliss of consumption.

Finally, I accepted that we had done something important. Our long journey, often arduous and contentious, had been worth it. We had made a valuable contribution to our world. Once again, the irony was not lost on me that by binding the breasts, we had unleashed the girls.

In 2017, Polly, Hinda, and I met in Los Angeles. On the occasion of the sports bra's fortieth anniversary, ESPN decided to fly us out to film a special, hosted by actress Eva Longoria, about our invention. Something interesting occurred shortly after our arrival. Polly and I were at breakfast in the hotel on the morning before filming when Hinda came in and asked if she might join us. We nodded and waved her toward one of the seats at our four-top.

I was surprised when Hinda then turned to me and said, "Lisa, I owe you an apology."

"For what?" I asked.

When she didn't respond right away, I continued. "I know what *I'd* like you to apologize for, but I want to hear what *you'd* like to apologize for . . ."

It was an odd moment, a strange reunion of we original three. A difficult conversation ensued wherein it became clear to me that we all craft our own realities, as we feel we must. We write our own stories.

I was expecting Hinda to apologize to Polly and me for that initial share purchase, for trying to erase Polly's early contributions, for yelling at me in the office constantly—things like that. But Hinda did not articulate any specific instances or items for which she wanted to apologize. When pressed about those things that haunted me, she claimed no memory. In fact, it never became clear to me exactly what Hinda wanted to apologize for. If Polly had not been there as a witness and a participant in some of our shared history, I might have thought I was crazy and making it up.

But really, did it matter?

Now, all these years later, the sports bra had changed not only us, but how women and girls everywhere were able to pursue comfort and athleticism.

As reported in the press, women were wearing sports bras in the Olympics, the Women's World Cup, and simply running down their own street after work to blow off steam. An entirely new industry had emerged, specifically designed to support the comfort and emerging physical and spiritual strength of women—athleisure. Why would the power struggles of we three women matter amid all this creation, emerging strength, and beauty?

Life is about the evolution of all of us—not just women, but humankind. It is about how we learn, grow, come to know—how we *become*. We evolve and change constantly.

We make an effort. We surrender. We dig in our heels. We get attached, tied down, tied into, or tied up. But every once in a while, we get unleashed. Or, better yet, we unleash ourselves—sometimes in the oddest, most counterintuitive ways possible—whether it's by partnering with a shadow teacher or by wearing a particular kind of bra.

I have a poignant memory: It was summer, 2001. The music squawked over the tinny speakers that were placed every few feet in order to overcome the ambient noise of engines, wind, and water. The ninety-degree heat beat onto the uncovered top deck, while the frenzied afternoon revelers danced in the relative shade of the second deck. Lake Champlain sparkled all around them. The Adirondacks slid by on one side, the Burlington and Shelburne waterfronts on the other. Few paid attention to this deep summer beauty. The final song came over the loudspeakers, its music galvanizing the dozens of partygoers. They formed a swaying, sweaty circle singing along to Queen's epic song, which had become their adopted anthem: "We are the champions. We are the champions. We are the champions . . . of the world . . ."

There were cheers, tears, and bleary laughter. One full-bellied and Hawaiian-shirted man with a grizzly, gray beard turned to hug the people on either side of him— one a purple-haired young woman in cutoffs and a T-shirt

that said, "I will survive" over a cartoon graphic of a figure hanging by one hand from a cliff. Mr. Hawaiian shirt's
next embrace recipient was a gray-permed, bespectacled
grandmother, who shyly hugged him back. They parted and
smiled ruefully at each other, catching their balance as the
big boat rocked on the swells.

It was odd to be here, watching this scene of celebration
that only partially masked the anxiety overshadowing the
partyers. I had left Jogbra, *chosen* to leave my company and
position almost a decade earlier, with no pomp or circumstance, as the saying goes. Yet for years, I had concealed and
tried to ignore the deep grief still attached to the particulars
of that leave-taking. Despite all my ensuing accomplish-
ments and positions elsewhere, the pain of that departure
lurked in my psyche. And now here I was at this event, at
this send-off, and it was triggering all that emotion.

I stood on that swaying boat thinking how I had ex-
cused and justified the severe and complete severing of ties
as necessary for all parties concerned—how, as a result, I'd
watched Jogbra from afar, with the pride of a distant parent,
as it and its community had continued to grow and evolve.
I had been only mildly interested to learn that as a result
of Playtex™ selling itself to Sara Lee™, Jogbra had become a
Champion™ brand. However, I had been very relieved when
they decided to build and move into a bigger building in
the same Vermont town, not far from the original Jogbra
headquarters at 13 Avenue D. It was only now, all these

years later, that Sara Lee™ was finally moving my company out of Vermont. And I was grateful to have been invited to witness this farewell party.

As this reminiscing brought tears to my eyes, I became self-conscious, aware of standing in the middle of time and watching this ripple effect of my long-ago ideas and actions. It was an extremely odd sensation. Alpha and omega. Beginning, middle, end—then *this* end. The business I had begun in 1977, sold in 1990, left in 1992, and kept distant tabs on for so long—rather like a mother monitoring her married child's journey through the world—was now closing down. While the inevitable job loss was major—many employees had worked for the company for more than fifteen years—that was not the only cause of the collective sorrow I was witnessing. Oh sure, the products would exist as part of a line in a division of its major corporate entity in a distant southern state. But—and it was this implicit "but" that powered the sorrow of the revelers around me—the company that was their *community* was dying. Everyone felt it was the end of an era. By November 3, 2001, Jogbra would be dead, wholly absorbed into the whale that is Sara Lee™ Corporation. The brand "Jogbra" was a tiny Jonah trying to survive in that corporation's large belly, and it had finally succumbed.

"Thank you. Excuse me, I just wanted to say thank you," a voice said beside me, disrupting my nostalgic reverie. "Thanks for nine years of good employment."

I stared into this stranger's quizzical face as she continued, "My name's Luella, and I've heard all 'bout you and I just wanted to meet you. You know, meet the inventor and say thanks." She reached for my drink-free hand and pumped it vigorously.

"Well, thank you, Luella! What is it that you do for Jogbra—er, Champion?"

"I'm in Quality Assurance! Been doin' that for many a time now. We just make sure that the goods is what they are meant to be."

"Well, thank you! Since I'm no longer around, I appreciate your making sure it's good stuff! What are you doing? Where are you going next, do you know?" This was the primary topic of conversation since the announcement had been made back in April.

Beaming, Luella responded, "Well, I'm from North Carolina originally, so I'm goin' home. Yes, I'm goin' back home, so I'm okay! Don't know if I'll work in some other place for the corporation or not. Don't know that for sure. But I'll be fine. I'm goin' home."

"Vermont must have been very different for you. The winters!"

"Oh yes! Oh, yes, them winters. It's been good, though. I'm glad I've been here. It's been nine good years. Yes. So, thank you. I just wanted to meet you and say thank you for inventing that bra." She snapped the straps of the Jogbra that peeked from beneath her T-shirt and laughed. "Thank you!" Then she moved off into the crowd, back toward the circle dancers.

Today, you only have to enter "sports bra images" into any internet search engine to see what my original Jock Bra has spawned. Her descendants are so many, so varied, so brightly colored, strappy, even sexy. Ironically, in some of these garments, "form follows function" has been disregarded in service to appearances. But most all have one thing in common: they are comfortable. And they are no longer only undergarments. Often, what is called a sports bra these days is worn as outerwear. In fact, the sports bra is credited with seeding the whole comfortable, casual fashion trend of athleisure.

Women are no longer wearing sports bras just for sports or to appear a certain way. They are primarily concerned with their own comfort and take it for granted that they may do so with their choice of sports bra. This is more significant than it might seem. Why? Because the historical purpose of the bra has formerly been to support (pun intended) the trends of fashion primarily—often at the sacrifice of comfort. Traditionally, the fashion industry has been more concerned with engaging the male gaze than with a woman's comfort. Think of corsets and boning. In the 1920s, it was the "little boy look" and breasts were minimized, sometimes to the point of being bound.

The 1930s and 1940s saw softer, more natural contours. Howard Hughes famously engineered a new kind of bra for Rosalind Russell, a cantilevered cup to lift up her glorious globes to the best (he thought) advantage.

By the 1950s, fashion deemed pointy breasts desirable, so bra cups were shaped to encapsulate the breast accordingly. Underwires, stiff boning placed under each breast, helped in the 1960s to "lift and separate." No, for most of history a bra's primary function was not about a woman's comfort—it was about making her breasts look trendy or her clothes hang correctly for that era's fashionable silhouette.

With the advent of the sports bra, however, function eclipsed fashion's predominance. In fact, the original Jogbra was rather unattractive, but it was supportive. It performed by helping to minimize breast movement during physical activity. There was no concern with the bra's look or the male gaze. Initially, long-term comfort was not even our foremost priority, as we did not expect sports bras to be worn for longer than the duration of a run or other exercise. The original Jogbra only needed to be comfortable under running conditions. It was never intended to be worn all day. That's funny to think about now.

The fact that the Jogbra has now created its own fashion meme is just the cycle coming full circle, as cycles do. Now, there are new companies springing up to design and manufacture "serious" sports bras. There is new fabric and production technology to facilitate clever solutions to old problems of support and comfort—especially for larger-breasted women, who need and want to be physically active without pain or hindrance. I love this. I think it is great!

It is important to note that when Hinda, Polly, and I entered the scene in 1977, there was little thought of the Jogbra growing into the feminist icon it has become. The sports bra liberated millions of women and girls across the globe from self-consciousness. And here we are, decades later, in a time when a whole generation now takes for granted that a comfortable bra is the norm, that those other sorts of bras are just for proms and weddings. In the future, just maybe—because that lavender lace sports bra sure looks pretty peeking out from under a prom dress—those old bras might be gone forever.

We've come a long way, baby.

26.
TODAY

"We shall not cease from exploration
And the end of all our exploring
Will be to arrive where we started
And know the place for the first time."
~ *T.S. Eliot*

A s I've said before, women's stories need to be told—their true stories, not the fairy tales or fame-glam stereotypes or strident melodramas still too prevalent today. In these times more than ever, the real stories of real women need to be told by the women who lived them—it's my new form of a "by women, for women" agenda for this era. My story about inventing the sports bra is one such story.

It was not easy for me to write this book—reading through my old journals, recalling painful incidents and some hard lessons. Revealing personal experiences beyond the public relations versions of events and then writing them down with the intent to share them was difficult.

"Nice girls" don't do such things. But I'm not a nice girl anymore; I'm a strong woman trying her best to be a compassionate, conscious being.

The tale of the troubled nature of my business partnership casts a contentious light on a sensitive aspect of women working together and the complicated and evolving paradigm of a significant facet of today's "sisterhood." I have always been a proponent of female bonding. Yet, consider this: sisterhood, brotherhood, *any*-hood—all are concepts that can invite polarization as much as they do bonding. Gender aside, we just need to be kinder to one another. We need to be thoughtful. We need to see the True Beauty in each other, which is so much bigger and more genuinely powerful than gender. What about a "humanhood"?

It took three humans—Lisa, Polly, and Hinda—to make the magic of Jogbra manifest, to create the right product at the right time and be able to deliver it to the population that needed and wanted it. I understand now that the mixture of each of our very different abilities and temperaments was a key ingredient in the alchemy of our success. Had we not each brought our particular abilities to the potion, the sports bra would not have been born in Burlington, Vermont in 1977 and gone on to become a thriving economic success for forty-plus years. Along the way, the Jogbra phenomenon did its bit for humanity by facilitating another phase of the women's liberation movement.

The business I helped to build was a perfect, albeit uncomfortable, classroom for me to learn about and confront my issues around fear and power, both real and imagined. At the time, I thought it a detour from my artistic purpose, only to find it has been the bootcamp for the rest of my journey.

Today, I am sitting on a porch overlooking Lake Champlain once again, but now I am on a different side of the lake, on a different curve of its shore. With binoculars, I can see across the broad, blue span to that cliff where my long-ago studio windowsill still stares out upon the water. My, how the perspective has changed. I don't struggle as much with my identity or question whether my Jogbra journey was worth it. Oh, it was—for so many reasons that are still unfolding to me.

I am, and have always been, a seeker—of solutions, of understanding, of evolutions, of True Beauty. Perhaps it is the seeking that is my life's purpose. I am *still* learning how to accept and integrate all the disparate bits of myself and fully embrace the evolving, authentic being that I am—artist, entrepreneur, friend, visionary cosmologist, spiritual healer—just a curious, glowing journeyer.

THE GUEST HOUSE

This being human is a guest house.
Every morning a new arrival.

A joy, a depression, a meanness,
some momentary awareness comes
as an unexpected visitor.

Welcome and entertain them all!
Even if they're a crowd of sorrows,
who violently sweep your house empty
of its furniture,
still, treat each guest honorably.
He may be clearing you out
for some new delight.

The dark thought, the shame, the malice,
meet them at the door laughing,
and invite them in.

Be grateful for whoever comes,
because each has been sent
as a guide from beyond.

~ Jalal al-Din Muhammad Rumi

ACKNOWLEDGMENTS

My challenge in writing this book was to decide which aspects of my story would be most relevant, intriguing, and illuminating for my reader. Was it the telling of the tale of invention and business success at a particular moment in women's history, or the personal memoir of my particular struggles therein? As I wrote, I realized it had to be all of it. Struggle is an intrinsic part of being human. The secret is that it is also an important, even necessary, tool for our personal healing and growth. I hope that by telling my story—of struggle, of becoming self-aware while pursuing the *conventional* definition of success—some light has been shed for others on their own paths. Yet I could not have told my story without a great deal of help. For their steady guidance, I'd like to thank my editor Michael Nolan and the amazing Kathy Meis, who always believed in the importance of this story and didn't let me get away with much. Their discernment, encouragement, and enthusiasm for this project has been an immense help. And to my early readers, especially Yvonne, Andy, and Priscilla, thank you for your perspective, honesty, support.

> *"Success is not final, failure is not fatal;*
> *it is the courage to continue that counts."*
> ~ *Winston Churchill*

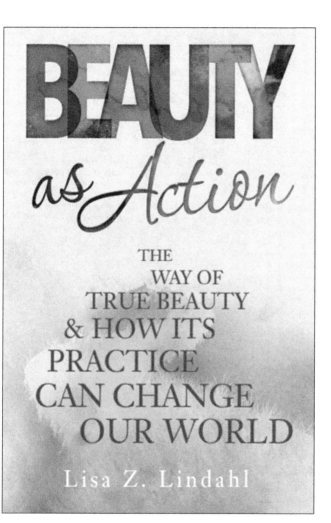

Available at bookstores and all
major online retailers.

Made in United States
Orlando, FL
10 September 2022

22198947R00183